LIVING
ON
INTUITION

Enriching Life Through Inner Guidance

by Robert Munster

Publishing Coach Deborah S. Nelson.
www.PublishingSOLO.com

TO ORDER ADDITIONAL COPIES OF THIS BOOK, CONTACT:

Over the Edge Publishing or purchase single copies from any online bookseller.

Acknowledgments

I am immensely grateful to the following people for their help in making this book come to life.

Frank Schnellert for the picture of the blue door on the cover.

Claudia Schwarz for the photo on About the Author.

Alyssa Monique for the incredible cover and interior design.

And, of course, my publishing coach, Deborah Nelson who has been both inspiring and patient with this fledgling author.

Dedication

This work is dedicated to those souls, both inhabiting bodies and those of the spirit world, who have guided me throughout my lifetime. i am un-endingly grateful for their love, protection and wisdom as they have led me in certain directions and provided me with a number of experiences that have shaped this incredibly interesting life.

Introduction

Many of us believe that intuition is a peculiar trait that is reserved for psychics, mediums or 'spiritual' people. Some individuals consider intuition to be a natural skill that we all possess and can access to assist us in every aspect of our lives.

During the major portion of my life, i have received bits and pieces of information from all corners of existence (people, animals, plants, minerals, spirits and especially from inside myself). After many of these messages proved themselves to have validity in my everyday life, i began trusting their guidance. In many instances, my situation immediately improved. During other times, it took a while before realizing how my life had changed. Either way, some kind of growth or wondrous thing happened.

This information need not come in big, booming voices or burning bushes; although those are not out of the question.

Many times it is a little whisper, a nudge or a hunch that, when listened to and acted upon, will the change the outcome of a situation. Intuition is a skill that needs building akin to that of physical exercise to strengthen our muscles.

Listening to and developing our intuition can most assuredly lead not only to helpful guidance in our daily lives, but also to a rich and meaningful life filled with beauty and wonder. So, go ahead – let go and listen to yourself and all that is around you. You may find that you really like what you discover.

Table of Contents

CHAPTER ONE

What is This Stuff Called Intuition?

According to Webster's dictionary, intuition is referred to as the following: 'insight'; 'to look at or in'; 'the act or faculty of knowing without the use of rational processes'; 'immediate cognition'; 'acute insight'. Let's throw in a couple of other words or phrases that mean something similar: inner guidance; inner wisdom; listening within; interspecies communication; hunches; nudges; clairvoyance or clairaudience.

No matter what we label it, this skill of listen-

ing is performed with something more than our minds. Intuition cannot be taught in books or classes. You have the natural ability within you already; it is not something you 'go out and get'. It is a matter of developing the skill of listening. That includes paying attention and hearing what is going on within and around you. Following are a few, simple examples of intuition.

Out of the blue, you start thinking of a person you've known in your past or present. Shortly thereafter that person either calls on the phone or sends you a note. Somehow this person came up on 'your screen' and, wham, there he or she is.

Let's say that you misplaced an item and realize that it is gone. Mentally and physically you trace all your previous steps and locations where you may have left the item. After a while, you give up. A little later you have a hunch of the whereabouts of the object.

Sure enough, you go look and there it is.

"The act or faculty of knowing without the use

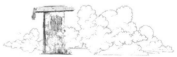

of rational processes" is very different from what we are accustomed to doing. Science, or the use of rational processes, is about as far away from intuition as one can be. In this physical world science has grown as the king of reality, even if a theory began as a hunch. According to the scientific rationale, something has to be proven; this means observed and repeated with the same results.

Once this is accomplished, something is thought to be true. Things or events that do not fit into that category are said to be untrue or not real.

If this is so, how does one explain the creation of a piece of music? Tunes, or rhythms, seem to appear out of nothingness; from somewhere that hasn't existed before. In a similar line of thought, how does a poem or ode find existence? Are these creations unreal?

How does one explain events that have no basis in reality yet prove themselves to be connected with day to day living?

For example: for two days in a row, Mary has

been thinking about a childhood friend that she hasn't seen in fifteen years. She feels an urgency to contact her old friend on the telephone. Once on the phone, her friend tells Mary that she has been very depressed for months. Mary spends one hour on the phone, simply listening to her.

At the end of the conversation, Mary's friend states that she felt completely alone and is very grateful that Mary has taken the time to listen to her.

Intuition, or inner wisdom, can appear to us in a number of ways. These include nudges, cues from other people, animals, plants or loved ones who have departed this life.

They can also come to us in the forms of dreams, both night and day; a line in a song or a casual phrase spoken by someone in the immediate area. Anything that captures our attention or is unusual in any way can provide us with useful information.

This can be as simple as the following event. One morning in Minneapolis, while preparing

to leave the hotel for the day, i heard a soft voice in my head say *take your hat and gloves with you.*

i looked out the window to a bright and sunny morning and thought, *Naw, i don't need them today.*

That afternoon the sky clouded over and the temperature dropped 20 - 30 degrees. It happened that i was working outside, all the while wishing that i had listened to that little piece of wisdom from the morning.

There are other times when listening to our intuition has a much more profound effect on our lives and/or the well-being of someone else around us. For example, while sitting at an intersection waiting for the light to turn green, i noticed an older man at the driver's seat in the car on my left.

We were both in thru traffic lanes. For some reason i grew anxious, feeling an urgency to take off as quickly as possible when the light changed. The signal turned green and i hit the gas.

15

My car was a foot or two ahead of the older man's vehicle as we entered the intersection. Just then, another car ran the red light from the right side and slammed into my right front bumper. The collision was just enough to change the direction of the oncoming vehicle, forcing it off to the right. That little alteration prevented the vehicle from t-boning the older man's car. The older gentleman drove down the street, none the worse.

My car had some minor damage to the front bumper. Both the other person and i were unharmed.

Later on, as i drove away and the shock wore off, i became aware that a greater harm (that of a possible serious accident) was averted. Then i understood why i felt the urgency to pull away from the traffic light so quickly.

The above examples were not planned. nor thought out in advance by any of the participants. They were 'acts of knowing without rational processing'. i believe that these acts happen much more frequently than is commonly

thought. Numerous experiences of my own and many others I've known have proven this to be so.

In fact, most of us have had such an experience or know of someone who has.

As you shall see throughout the pages of this book, the range of usefulness of following intuition can be quite broad.

These can be as simple enhancements of day to day living, as profound as changing the course of someone's life or protection from disaster and sometimes death.

i sincerely hope that you find something meaningful within these pages.

CHAPTER TWO

How Intuition Helps in Our Daily Lives

Sometimes i feel as though i have an ace up my sleeve. That card is intuition and without it, i don't know how i would survive. i am fairly intelligent and perceptive, however, i seem to be led by the nose into better situations that i could possibly dream up on my own. Maybe it is the mere fact that i simply pay attention. Somewhere along the path i have grown to trust what messages come my way.

i honestly cannot say when this happened.

Seems to me it has always been that way. i guess if something succeeds again and again, it becomes part of our repertoire.

Inner guidance, or intuition, appears in so many different forms. A common method for me is hearing. This can be a whisper or a booming voice from within, a phrase from another person that 'lights up' or a direct communiquè from an animal, dolphin, plant and/or mineral form. Sometimes it is a matter-of-fact directive from someone who does not inhabit a physical form.

Another regular way for me to receive messages is via my dreams, both night-time and day dreams. As with hearing, some dreams are loud and clear, while others require some deciphering. Dreams can be a gold mine of information and guidance.

Many people receive guidance through sight; they see things clearly and glean information from their visual worlds. Others simply sense things – they can feel their way through daily life relying on their gut feelings to keep them on

course. i have met a number of individuals who had powerful skills in these areas. Still yet another group of people just 'know things.' There is a skill that someone termed 'direct perception.' The person doesn't need to hear, feel or see; he or she simply knows. i have experienced this myself on a few occasions and hold this talent in very high regard.

An individual may possess natural talent in one or all of the above areas.

One skill may be stronger at one point in someone's life, then change or blend with another. Often, a person's intuitive skills may appear following a near-death or some other life-altering experience. Whichever sense we use to gather information, intuition can help and support us in many ways to improve the quality of our daily lives.

AN UNLIKELY WAY TO FIND A HOUSE

i had to find a new house, as i was about to lose the one i was living in. i spent several afternoons searching different local communities within the Salt Lake area to no avail. Late one

afternoon, tired and discouraged, i was driving home from another fruitless search.

Without any warning or guidance, the wheel of my truck started turning to the right. i thought, *what is going on here?* i assisted by completing the turn. i hung on to the wheel, keeping the vehicle going forward. Two blocks up a small hill, the wheel started to turn left. Ok, i thought, *something special is happening here because i have never experienced anything like this before.* About two houses in from the corner the truck started slowing down, so i pulled over to the side of the road.

My attention was drawn to a house on the left that just so happened to have a 'for sale' sign on the lawn.

Unbelievable, i thought to myself. Ok, my truck, or whatever, led me to this spot. i took down the number, promising myself that i would call that night.

i told the realtor that i was interested in looking at the home. The next day we met. The house

fit everything i wanted and needed. i liked it right down to the garden space in the back yard which overlooked the valley. i told the man that i was in a rather awkward economic situation. As part owner in five other properties that held all my liquid assets in check, i couldn't possibly see how i could come up with the financing. He convinced me to put down a small deposit, saying to me, "Let's just give it a shot. You've got nothing to lose." My inner voice said *OK, go ahead*.

Within forty-five days, all my finances cleared, providing me with just enough money to purchase and move into my new home. Did i require external assistance on that one or what? Intuition can be so exacting and synchronistic that i am always amazed when something like this takes place.

THE FIREPLACE

i spent two years building a massive fireplace. It must weigh well over 8-10 tons consisting of firebrick, regular red brick, specialized concrete hardware innards and hundreds of field stones

23

gathered from around the country. i hired a man who was invaluable during this task; he was a genius at building. After completing 3⁄4 of the heater, he figured that i knew enough to finish the rest by myself. i was on my own.

At about the same time, i decided that my self-built house needed to have a second floor. Up went the posts and beams necessary to make the house a two-story structure.

i purchased sixty four hemlock 2"x 12"s from a local man who used horses to drag the trees out of the woods and, then cut them into 26 foot lengths. The things were heavy and long.

i had no idea how i would secure them onto the beams. i had never built a house before; only a two room sauna and remodeled a bathroom.

At the end of one work day, i stood by the fireplace and said aloud, "i don't know what to do here. If i am to build this house, i need help." i grew accustomed to asking such things throughout the entire building project. It hadn't failed me before.

That very evening while pondering this dilemma, i had a vision. An image of a triangular metal box with holes filled my mental screen. i thought, *now where on earth am I going to find something like that?*

On my way into town the following day, i received a nudge to take an alternate route. Lo and behold, there on the back country road was a metal fabrication shop. i stepped inside.

There were all kinds of specially created metal works and wrought iron hanging on the walls. i told the owner what i saw in my head. He said, "No problem, how big do you want them?"

We discussed their function while he drew pictures on paper. He suggested making a few adjustments to the holes which would allow me to set the boxes and lug bolts right into the cement at the top of the stove. Not only would that allow me to join the hemlock floor joists solidly onto the stove, but also give me the leeway to adjust each piece of wood to the correct level. i ordered sixteen of them.

The time came to install my special boxes. They were easy to set into the cement and adjust. As i was about to drive the first nail through the side of the box and into the wood, i heard that little voice say, "Don't do that; think about the wood, the stove and the temperature." i stepped back to think. i thought as I looked at all the pieces involved. *Wood being that close to the stove will expand.*

When it is cold (and it does get cold in Maine), the wood will contract. The floor joists are nailed to the outside wall posts. What if i left the wood free to move with the temperature? That would prevent the outside walls of the house from being pushed and pulled every time the temperature changed.

This made perfect sense to me. i could never have figured this out on my own.

Contractors and carpenters have visited my house. Most of them are curious about how i attached the floor joists to the fireplace (among other things). i ask them if they really want to know.

If they say yes, i tell them that a little voice inside my head told me what to do. Typically they laugh.

THE PHONE

i cannot recount how many times i had a hunch to call someone. Once i did they tell me they were just thinking of calling me or that i have been on their minds for the last few days. Often i call people to tell them a certain phrase that i am told to say without even considering it. The person will inform me how important it was to hear those particular words. Other times i feel that someone close to me is having a rough time, so i call or e-mail to say, "i was just thinking of you and i want you to know that i love you." The reply is typically, "Your words really helped me today; how did you know?"

The reverse is also true. An image of a person enters my mental screen or a sense of someone tickles my psychic antennae and a few minutes later that person is on the phone. It has happened so many times in the past that i might even answer the phone with "Hi," and his or

her name. "How did you know it was me?" No, i don't have caller id.

Next time the phone rings, try guessing who is calling before you answer.

SOME OF MY FAVORITES

There haven't been many ocean swells coming out of the north this winter. That means a lack of good waves at one particular breaking spot here on the island. Whenever a solid swell arrived, i went to 'the spot' to check it out. No good. There was too much surge to the surf or the swell had too much east to it or the wind wasn't right. This went on for most of the winter. Now, don't get me wrong; there have been plenty of good waves at other spots, but not 'the spot.'

One particular day, around mid-morning, the little voice said, "Put a board in the truck and go to 'the spot.' So, i did exactly that. Once there, i discovered that no one was in the water.

The morning sky was an endless blue, the wind

lightly off-shore, the waves head high and glassy. Out i paddled with a grin on my face. i had the place to myself for over an hour. The wind came up, the tide changed, i rode a wave in and paddled to the shore, a grin plastered on my face still.

i am project oriented most of the time. i wake in the morning, do my physical and spiritual exercises, eat and start on my list for the day (that is, of course, after surfing). While home in Maine, my list is long enough to keep ten people busy for a month. i typically go from one task to the next to the next and to the next before i realize that i should eat or rest for a bit. The summer days in Maine are long so it is common for me to eat dinner around 8:30 or 9:00 at night. Then it's 'lights out', unless of course it is a clear night and the stars are prime for gazing.

In the middle of this 'project frenzy', the little voice regularly makes itself known. It may say, "Tomorrow morning, you need to play golf or bike or kayak before anything else." Every time i listen and follow through, i find myself grateful for doing so.

29

The funniest times are when the voice tells me to "Go sit down."

A few years ago i placed two chairs (one extra for company) by the side of a stream/beaver dam deep in the woods near the house. After twenty minutes of sitting quietly and trying to be invisible, the animals return to their regular activity. It is common for me to witness the movement of deer and birds around the water source. Of course, by that time, i am completely relaxed and rejuvenated. It works so well. All i need to do is listen and act.

Another of my favorites is when inner guidance whispers in my ear telling me to 'pay attention' or 'open your heart'.

Each and every time i hear one of these phrases i know that something very special is about to take place. And, without fail, it does.

These little events happen all the time. The more we pay attention to them, the more they become part of our everyday life.

At some point they create a certain fabric in our lives that is natural and commonplace. In fact, after a while, we come to expect them as naturally as we expect the earth beneath us or the air we breathe. Our lives take on a kind of magical element.

CHAPTER THREE

Protection

There are numerous times when we are pre-sented with the opportunities to avoid painful and/or disastrous events. We are given these chances via nudges, little inner voices, clues in the environment or, at times, big booming voices. No matter in what form they appear, the messages are there for our protection. Haven't you ever had the 'feeling' that going to a certain place or engaging in a certain activity was not going to end well?

Did you follow that guidance? If not, what hap-pened?

This chapter contains experiences and events that have either prevented something bad from happening or literally saved my life or the life of another person.

THROUGH THE FLOOR

It was late afternoon and i'd been working on the house all day. Walking over the 4'x8' sheets of plywood that acted as temporary flooring on the second story, i looked down and noticed a pile of wood in the area where i used to split cedar logs. It was stacked a foot high and adjacent to a round slab that i cut wood upon. The hand axe sat on top of that.

Instantly i heard inside my head, "You need to clean that pile up right now." i remember thinking that I was too tired to listen when the voice said, "Do it now!"

i dragged my exhausted body through the motions and cleaned the entire area which was close to the stairs. At one point i thought that i was finished. "Not so, clean it all", said the voice. OK, OK, and i did.

The next day while working upstairs with my brother, i needed a tool for a specific task. i started walking towards the stairwell and *Wham!* The piece of plywood was not completely supported and i fell through the floor joists slamming my chest against a 2"x12" rock hard timber.

Once through the floor and onto the cement flooring downstairs, the wind was knocked out of me. It took me a moment to recover from the shock when i realized that i landed exactly where the axe, round splitting slab and all the cut pieces of wood were stacked the day before.

Not only did i escape those potentially harmful objects, but also missed the corner of the stairs by inches.

i fractured a rib and skinned my arms, but avoided breaking any of my extremities. i fell about ten feet down to the cement floor without a major injury. i sat there for a few moments grateful as could be for listening to and following the guidance from the previous afternoon.

LEAVING BOLIVIA

My wife called the airline to confirm our flight to Peru and was informed of a delay of two hours or more. Thinking that we had extra tourist time, we considered taking the bus to the airport instead of a cab. That way we could see more of La Paz before flying away.

We dragged our suitcases down to the local square where we could hop on a bus. After two minutes at the bus/taxi stand i felt a strong necessity to get to the airport. i screamed to my wife, "Grab that taxi RIGHT NOW!" Off to the airport we went, urging the driver to be quick about it.

i explained to my spouse that the inner voice was so strong i could not ignore it.

Once at the airport, we jumped out of the cab, grabbed our bags and rushed to the airline counter. They informed us that our flight was due to leave in ten minutes. We freaked, they freaked. The man behind the counter said, "Come now, hurry." We ran at full speed dragging our suit-

cases behind us in order to keep up with the guy. He hurried us past and through customs within ten seconds and then on to the gate.

When we arrived at the gate, the woman motioned for us to follow her, suitcases and all. They were closing the door of the plane as the lady screamed, "Stop!" The stewardess opened the door, took our luggage and escorted us to a pair of seats in first class. The plane left the gate immediately.

It took thirty minutes or more for both of us to catch our breath and calm down.

With the help of inner guidance we flew away from La Paz, Bolivia as originally scheduled.

IMPOSSIBLY CLOSE ENCOUNTER

Late one night on my way to Minneapolis, i was driving on the New York Thruway. It was middle to late October with the temperature just below freezing. i drove the middle lane; another car was in the passing lane and both of us approached a semi on the right. The vehicle on my

left nudged ahead of me as i started to pass the back end of the eighteen-wheeler.

Suddenly, the semi started to jackknife, the cab entering my lane. The car on the left went into a spin, also crowding into the middle lane. i knew a serious accident was about to happen when, suddenly, the entire scene went into slow motion. A voice inside my head said keep going, don't react. I maintained my speed and direction as i watched the vehicles coming towards me from both sides. By all physical rights they should have collided with me.

However, my car squeaked through the opening.

Once free of both the car and truck, things returned to regular speed. i looked into my rear view mirror just in time to witness the two vehicles smash into each other. i slowed down and pulled over to the side of the highway. By the time i recovered from the shock (2-3 minutes), police cars were on the scene. i continued on my way only until i found a rest area where i slept for the remainder of the night.

The next day i heard on the radio that there were a number of accidents on the Thruway due to 'black ice' on the roadways. To this day, i believe that 'something' or 'someone' was present during that event which saved me from a catastrophe.

THREE IN A ROW

i left my friends' house early one morning on my way out of Massachusetts, heading west. i had a funny feeling in the pit of my stomach that something was going to happen on the trip that day. The nudge i received was to 'pay close attention' to traffic.

Within minutes of entering onto the highway, i came upon a van which had crashed into the guard rail apparently a few moments earlier. The driver exited from the vehicle looking a bit shaken. 'Pay attention' the voice repeated itself. Approximately thirty minutes later another accident occurred on the opposite side of the highway. Police cars were just arriving on site. Again I heard that little voice inside my head, 'pay attention'. *OK, alright, i hear you.*

Another half an hour down the road the highway joined I-84 into Hartford. The traffic was relatively light for 10:30 am.

i finally calmed down thinking that the worst was behind me. Suddenly my awareness was heightened as i noticed an SUV weaving in and out of traffic behind me. i immediately slowed from 70 down to 55ish.

About a hundred yards in front of me the SUV and a sedan collided as they both swerved into the middle lane at the same time. The sedan veered sharply off the right side of the highway while the SUV went into a roll. It spun over three times before landing on its side and into the median cement wall. i, and the other vehicles nearby, reacted by slowing down and steering around the overturned SUV, thus preventing any further accidents or complications.

For the remainder of my way to and through Hartford, i remained in a super state of alertness as i maintained a 'white knuckle' grasp on the steering wheel. Once the city traffic abated, i reflected on the experience.

Would it have made any difference if i hadn't received those nudges to 'pay attention'? i really don't know, however, the probability of my being involved in the accident with the SUV and sedan could have been much higher.

COMMON STORIES

Many times we hear stories from a friend or someone else who had a premonition about not going on an airplane, bus or to a social happening (sports event or concert). Either they have followed the message or have been somehow physically prevented from making it there (flat tire, heavy traffic, car won't start, etc.). Later on they discovered that some tragedy had befallen the event.

Stories such as this appear in the media on occasion. A few years ago there was a huge mine that collapsed in South America, i think it was. The event was awash with such incredible stories.

The one that affected me the greatest was the one about the butterfly. Two men were deep

in the mines, maybe as much as a quarter of a mile in, when they saw a butterfly. They were amazed that the creature could even live that far underground. Both men felt a nudge to follow the butterfly which eventually led them out of the mine to safety. Their story touched people around the globe.

Tales and events such as these inspire us to believe in the power of intuition, inner guidance or whatever one wishes to call this extraordinary stuff that appears in our lives for our protection and benefit.

CHAPTER FOUR

Guidance at Work

Right from the start of my career i learned how to listen to patients/clients in order to discover what they needed to improve their situation. As an occupational therapy aide, i quickly learned that expertise combined with the ability to build a rapport created a powerful therapeutic milieu. During the first few years of practicing as a registered therapist, i noticed it didn't matter that a therapist had a half a dozen initials behind his or her name.

If that person did not connect in a meaningful way with the patient, there was very little motivation or positive energy in the therapy session.

i have witnessed a janitor inspire more motivation out of a patient than some therapists with Masters degrees or PhDs. At one hospital where i developed a number of programs, i loved watching a therapy assistant run an exercise session. She could get those patients to do anything she asked. They loved her because she truly respected and liked them. She touched them inwardly. And you know – they all grew stronger and more independent.

Some therapists are very adept at learning what is important to their clients and quickly build a rapport and therapeutic regime to help the person get what they want. It is not about the expertise. It is about the client. It is in this area that intuition helped me become a more efficient therapist for over thirty five years.

i owe my level of expertise to clients training me along the way.

The following experiences are but a scant few where intuition and inner guidance have led me to serve other people in times of need. The names, of course, are fictitious.

ONE OF MY FIRST PATIENTS

Mrs. Campbell was the name on the referral for 'activities of daily living.' i found the room and located her. i introduced myself, "Hi, Mrs. Campbell, my name is Bob and i'm here to get you up and ready for breakfast.

Let's get you to the bathroom and then washed and dressed."

Her back straightened a bit as she replied, "Young man, you will do no such thing."

i didn't know what to do. i thought for a moment until I received an inspiration.

Then, I knelt down on one knee and said, "Now, Mrs. Campbell, when is the last time a good looking young man knelt at your feet?" She cracked up. That's how we started her therapy.

i worked with Mrs. C for four weeks or so every Monday through Friday, twice a day. She told me what she needed to accomplish in order to become independent enough to return home. We both worked hard to make that happen.

The day came for her to leave rehab. Once she finished with her personal care (independently i might add), she asked me to sit down for a moment.

She told me, "Sonny, you are a very nice young man. One day, after you blink your eyes a few thousand times, you will be right where I am now. You may think you have forever, but you don't. Always remember to live from your heart and make your own dreams come true. No one else can or will do this for you. Thank you for all your help. Now, let's get out of here. I'm going home today."

Her words have stayed with me and guide many of my life's decisions for nearly forty years.

IMAGERY AND COPD

My first real job as a registered occupational therapist included treating patients with many types of disabilities plus developing new programs and building a department. Another new staff member, a physician, transferred from the well-known Rancho los Amigos Rehabilitation Hospital in Los Angeles.

It wasn't long before he introduced himself to me, stating that he wanted to coordinate a twenty-one day therapy program for clients with Chronic Obstructive Pulmonary Disease (COPD).

Dr. David described the program he envisioned including regular therapy for building strength, endurance and independence plus instruction in relaxation and self-monitoring that the clients could employ at home.

Most COPD patients, he told me, kept recycling through hospitalizations until they eventually died. He wanted to break that cycle, reduce the number of hospital stays and record any chang-

es that we could utilize for future research. He appeared quite innovative and open-minded. i told him i would love to be involved with such a program.

He referred his first client to me, Mr. J. We began with short, frequent exercise sessions. i recorded his blood pressure, pulse, number of respirations per minute plus other observable data before, during and after each treatment session. One morning i noticed that Mr. J was excessively short of breath and unable to perform any physical exercise. i thought to myself, what do i do now? i heard a soft voice in my head say, "Do some exercises using his imagination."

OK, i thought, *What can i have him do?* The answer came immediately – *Have him pretend to walk up a few flights of stairs.*

i explained to Mr. J what i wanted him to do. As soon as he started, he gasped for breath. i stopped him and explained that we were just pretending to walk up stairs. He resumed the exercise and, again started rapid, shallow

breathing. *Wow, this is interesting, i thought.*

For the next few days i encouraged Mr. J. to continue to imagine walking up and down stairs with the goal of climbing five sets, each one containing ten steps.

This we combined with instruction in abdominal breathing and muscular relaxation exercises. His vital signs began to normalize. The physician informed me that Mr. J.'s arterial blood gases were improving. He said, "Keep doing whatever it is you are doing with him. It's working."

Within a month we had four or five new clients going through the program. i increased the goal to ten flights of stairs with each one of them.

One of our patients was a smoker of many years. The doc told me that her lung tissue had grown fibrotic (hard and stiff). One afternoon during her therapy session i received a nudge to try something different. *Why not take her down into her lungs to have her see what they look like?* i told Mrs. D my plan. She agreed.

Once i guided her down the airways and into one of the lobes, she stated that it was dark in there. i advised her to look up and pull the chain attached to the light bulb.

She did so and let out a big sigh. "Oh my God, the walls are covered with gooey black stuff." i asked her what needed to be done with the stuff. She replied, "Get it out of here so I can breathe." i told her to look around for some kind of tool that she could use.

She found a pick axe and went to work pulling the black substance from the walls of her lungs. After a moment or two Mrs. D asked, "How do I get this stuff out of here? This place needs some fresh air." i encouraged her to find a door handle and open the door. As soon as she did so, Mrs. D released a huge breath and stated, "Ah, that feels so good."

We spent the remainder of the treatment time cleaning the black goo from the walls and tossing it out the door while letting fresh air and sunshine into her lungs. Between the both of us, we stumbled upon a remarkable insight. Peo-

ple can have major input into their own healing processes.

Doctor Dave was amazed at the positive changes in her vital signs and blood gases. We were on our way to creating a new and innovative treatment program blending medicine with imagery and imagination techniques.

One day the doc approached me asking me if i could use my techniques to help a patient during abdominal surgery. He told me that the client was a 'bleeder', which could seriously hamper the surgery. i said, "Of course, i will try, but first of all, you must take me through what will specifically take place, step by step, during the operation." He took time that very afternoon to describe the procedure to me.

The surgery was scheduled in two weeks. Every day i led the client through the surgical procedure, all the while reminding him to envision healthy tissues and no internal bleeding. We were all a bit anxious when the day came. Late that morning the doctor sought me out to tell me that the operation was a huge success – no

internal hemorrhaging at all. The patient was doing fine.

During the mid-70s, the term 'Holistic Healing or Holistic Medicine' was not acceptable in the general medical or public arenas.

Those who practiced alternative methods were viewed as charlatans and quacks. There was no scientific proof that they worked. However, you couldn't convince Dr. Dave or me of that fact.

We had plenty of proof; our clients got better.

THE RAILROAD MAN

i received a referral for "Functional Transfer Training" for a man, let's call him Roscoe. He was a retired railroad man and about as gruff a character as you could find. His diagnosis was terminal stage cancer. He appeared withered and frail, a sunken image of a vigorous, spunky, 'not to be messed with' tough man.

Even his language was rough, crude and to the point.

When i introduced myself and described why i was in his room, he told me that it didn't matter what the hell i did. *Didn't i know he was dying?*

i informed him that his doctor wanted me to make sure he could get to the bathroom and into a chair for meals. He stated, "I don't give a damn what you do, so have at it." For some reason i replied with, "Why don't i just show up and we can tell each other lies?" It caught him off guard – he smiled.

Over the next couple of weeks i appeared at Roscoe's bedside twice a day and convinced him to get out of bed for short while. Just moving from the bed to the chair drained much of his energy. Once he caught his breath, i asked him to tell me another story about railroad life. That's all it took; he had hundreds of them; many of the stories from the 'good old days' of railroading. His face brightened with every tale he told.

i discovered that he smoked two packs of Lucky Strikes a day for years. His favorite beer was Coors. Every single day he told me, "What I wouldn't give for a smoke and a beer."

Day by day Roscoe grew weaker. He knew he was dying; he wanted it to happen quickly. He'd say, "The last thing I want is to be a burden to Anne (his wife)". One Thursday afternoon, on a hunch, i asked Roscoe if there was any one last thing he wanted to do. i had in mind something like call an old friend or clean up some-unfinished business. He replied, "Go to a nice restaurant, have a steak, a couple of beers and a smoke." *Hmmm*, I thought.

i marched off in search of the head nurse. i gave her my spiel about Roscoe making his last wish known. To my surprise, she said, "Do it, but remember, should you get into an accident, you are not covered." "That's fine with me," i replied. i suddenly felt a sense of urgency so i stated, "we better do it tomorrow; i don't think we have much time left."

The next day at noon i arrived at Roscoe's room. He was dressed and ready to go wearing a cat - eating grin and a sparkle in his eye. We drove to a nice local restaurant a few blocks away. The transfers in and out of the car and into the wheelchair were difficult because he didn't

have much strength and readily fatigued. We managed with the help of a few choice phrases, railroad style.

Once situated at our table he ordered a medium rare steak and a bottle of Coors. The look on his face when he took that first slug of ice cold beer was priceless. Roscoe was a happy man. Thirty minutes later, after one and a half beers, he barely finished a quarter of his steak dinner and grew tired and short of breath. He relented that he was ready to go back to the hospital.

On the return trip i pulled the car into a little strip mall and parked. i opened the glove compartment and produced a fresh pack of Lucky Strikes. i informed him that this was against every hospital policy ever written but if he really wanted one, now was the time to 'light up.' "Hell, yes", he replied. "These things are probably what are killing me now, but this is the way I want to go."

He was able to smoke about half of a cigarette before putting it out. "That's some nasty stuff," he said.

He was completely spent by the time we got him undressed and back into bed. He thanked me about ten times for taking him out. By then it was late Friday afternoon as i was preparing to leave for the weekend. i said, "Well Roscoe, that was fun; i'll see you on Monday." The look on his face said otherwise, so i walked to the side of his bed and stood there.

This rough and tough old railroad man took my hand and held it. He said, "These past couple of weeks you have been like a son and a good friend to me. i have never said this to another man before. i love you. If you ever tell anyone I said this, I will come back and haunt you."

i told him that it was an honor to get to know him even for such a short time. i squeezed his hand, said my goodbye and left the room.

i cried while writing his last progress note. Before i left the unit, i told the head nurse that Roscoe thought that he was going to leave that night. She looked at me as though i had six heads.

That following week everyone on that unit kept staring at me. How on earth did i know that Roscoe was going to die on Friday night? i didn't, Roscoe did.

THE DEBUT

The diagnosis was *anorexia nervosa*. Janet was a young woman who appeared a bit wiry and jumpy. i guess that is why i received a referral for 'arts and crafts – keep patient occupied'. This was the referring physician's first case of anorexia and she wanted to go 'by the book.' So, of course, i did my research. i discovered that the abnormal symptoms that accompany this disorder typically start with some sort of emotional trauma.

Janet and i met each day; we brought games and other crafts to the visiting room. While we engaged in these activities, we talked about where she came from, where she grew up and what she liked to do with her spare time. i noticed that she kept looking at the piano in the room and averting her eyes as though something wasn't quite right. One afternoon i asked

her if she ever played. She told me the story of her and the piano.

She played ever since she was a little girl of four. Her mother encouraged her to practice at least two to three hours per day. She confided in me that she felt pushed to practice and perform better when all she wanted to do was go outside and play with her friends. On the one hand, she wanted to be a 'normal kid' and on the other, she wished to please her mom.

Two years prior to her hospitalization, Janet was scheduled for her debut. This event would decide whether or not a famous school of music opened its doors to her.

Janet grew very anxious as she told me how she froze on stage, unable to perform her piece of music. She ran off stage that afternoon ashamed and embarrassed and hasn't been able to touch a piano since. She cried.

i sat with her until she regained her composure then escorted her back to her room. i told Janet, "These things happen in our lives and the best

we can do is make it through to the other side."

I left Janet and went to the nursing station to write my daily progress note stating what transpired. i made a special effort to be concise and clear because the doc wanted to keep on top of her case. i also discussed that afternoon's session with the head nurse, stating that the piano debut may be the precipitating event for her disorder. She agreed with me.

Over the next few days i followed my hunch by moving our session closer and closer to the piano in the visiting room. One afternoon Janet started talking about the piano and how she loved to play certain pieces of classical music.

Moved by an inner nudge i went over and sat on the piano bench. i invited her over and, to my surprise, she sat down next to me. i asked if she would like to play something.

She said, "I can't." i blurted out, "OK then, check this out." i began banging on the keyboard creating a God-awful racket. In less than one minute, she grabbed my hands saying,

"Stop. Alright, I'll play something."

For twenty or thirty minutes Janet produced some beautiful classical pieces. Her face was aglow, her breathing deep and full. Then, for some reason, i asked her if there was a piece of her own music that she had composed.

She played something so moving i cried. Her entire countenance changed as though some huge burden was lifted from her being. She thanked me profusely as we walked back to her room.

The head nurse, upon seeing a new Janet, asked me, "What happened? She looks completely different." i related the story as it occurred. We chatted for a few moments about this breakthrough in Janet's case. Before leaving i reminded the nurse that sometimes there is a 'rebound' phenomenon that follows such a drastic event. "Janet may have a rough night; she has been through quite an afternoon."

i arrived at the hospital the next day. As soon as i walked in the front door, the Human Resources director intercepted me. He informed me that

i was fired. He told me that i went against the doctor's orders. He then directed and followed me to my office in order to gather my belongings before leaving the grounds.

i was shocked.

Later that afternoon, the head nurse telephoned to let me know exactly why i was terminated. She stated that Janet stayed up most of the night playing the piano.

In the morning she refused to take any more medication and requested to leave the hospital against medical advice. The doctor was furious that i tampered with her patient's care and made sure that i would not do it again.

Sometimes we entrench ourselves so deeply in empirical information we believe that it is the only truth. At those times we easily forget that the real truth lies within the people we are attempting to serve.

As for Janet, i often wonder what happened with her. For those few, brief moments i watched her

come alive again. That was a gift for me.

WHILE YOU'RE AT IT

We spend approximately one third of our daily lives at work. What a great opportunity to practice building our intuitive, skills. If we believe in what we do we are more than likely utilizing our natural talents while employed.

Intuition or inner wisdom tends to focus upon our natural skills to bring about higher states of consciousness no matter where we are.

Over the next week or two while at work, pay close attention to your immediate environment and the people around you. What do they have to tell you without saying one word? Listen for words or phrases that jump out at you and follow your hunches even in the littlest of events, like what to have for lunch or *'What would happen if I?'*...

And most of all, follow that wisdom even if you don't understand it.

CHAPTER FIVE

Help in Times of Need

i always need help. Somehow i get myself into situations, or events present themselves, that appear impossible to resolve. Almost every time i've needed help with something in my life, it has arrived at the precise moment of necessity. Even those instances where assistance was not apparent, some form of guidance appeared to help me find a way to manage a challenging situation. Therein holds a key for me: not a bail out, but an assist.

A man whom i hold in the highest regard said

that "there is no spiritual welfare but there is always assistance no matter where you find yourself in life. You have to be willing to do your part and spirit will help you find a way."

ON STAGE

Back in the mid 70's i accepted a lead role in a five act play. The people who asked seemed convinced that i was the appropriate one for the role and that little voice inside said, "Do it." i consented.

There was one minor catch – the performance was scheduled in six weeks.

The next few days i spent two to three hours each night going over the script. There were so many lines to remember; how on earth was i to accomplish this? i felt like i was 'in over my head.' i started to panic which only made things worse. Late that night, after the kids were in bed and my studying was completed, i sat on the living room couch considering my plight. i drove the freeway to and from my internship every day, worked all day, then fed and played

with the kids before putting them to bed and doing my homework for the Masters' program. *What was i going to do?* i didn't want to back out from my agreement, yet honestly thought i couldn't do it.

The voice spoke softly in my head, "Why don't you tape the lines? Tape everybody's lines." Wow, great idea, I thought. i taped everyone's lines except for mine.

i listened to the tape while i drove the hour trip on the freeways twice a day. Anytime i prepared a meal or watched the kids outside, i practiced my lines. After three or four weeks i had the entire play committed to memory. Then i started working on my emotional tones and inflections as i dropped into the role of the character. i found it fascinating to emulate an archeologist who finds ancient scrolls while diving off the coast of California (they actually filmed me).

When the night of the performance arrived, i let myself go. There was magic on the stage as the character discovered ancient truths hidden within the scrolls. Whenever anyone forgot

their lines, i cued them with a couple of words and they responded with ease. The play ended with another film clip. The archeologist delivered the secret scrolls to a master who waited at a gazebo on top of a long flight of steps. i lived and i learned.

THE AIRPORT

My flight out of Miami was cancelled. The airline workers directed me to the service counter. The line was long and slow; Claudia left to go through customs and check her bags. i kept her carry on because she had a ton of baggage. Finally my turn came to arrange another flight.

The clerk informed me that my only option was a flight out of Ft. Lauderdale. In order to do this i had to hop on an airport shuttle within 30 minutes. That was the only way to make the flight. One little issue remained; i had my sweetie's carry-on luggage and didn't know where she was other than some international area.

i started to walk in the direction she left while dialing her cell number. She answered but had

no idea where she was other than a check-in area waiting in line. She couldn't even give me directions. Well, this was a fine mess. My head wanted to panic but i held that in check and tuned into Claudia's image. At each intersection i asked inwardly, *Which way do I go?*

Time was running out but i kept following the nudges to go this way, then that way. i came upon an escalator and the voice said, "Down."

Once on the escalator and descending, her presence grew very strong. As i glanced around the terminal, there she was, putting her luggage onto the x-ray ramp. i approached her from the back saying, "Well, hello there, do you come around here often?" Her face registered astonishment. "How on earth did you find me?" "Radar," i replied.

A BETTER BACK

For a number of years, my back was a problem. Multiple accidents and injuries plagued my spinal column leaving me in pain.

Five auto accidents, including two hard rear-end collisions, falling off the back of a motor-cycle at 40 mph, falling from a military truck in Vietnam, driving my motorcycle off an 18 ft cliff, hitting the bottom of the ocean twice nearly crushing my cervical spine and bouncing off trees and reefs. Including near drowning events, i have brushed against death's door well over fifty times.

Bodies don't fare well with this kind of activity. Four or five times a year, my back went out causing me excruciating pain. The treatment approach was fairly straightforward: on the couch for 24-36 hours, crawling to the bathroom, then chiropractic sessions every day for five days in a row. The following week it was three treatments, the next week twice, thereafter once a week for a few weeks. Throughout this regime, i moved through my days very gingerly in order to keep the pain at a minimum. For the neck injuries, a cervical traction home device was necessary.

This went on for over five years. i began asking inwardly for some help in dealing with this

condition. One day while driving north from Salt Lake for my meeting with a skilled nursing facility management staff, i heard a clear voice from inside tell me to drive the secondary road that runs north along the mountains. i had a couple of hours until the meeting, so off i went, up the country road.

i followed a nudge to turn into a small park overlooking the Great Salt Lake, thinking this was a nice place to have my lunch.

i parked the car and found a grassy knoll to settle upon. As soon as i sat down and relaxed a bit, the voice of an inner guide said, "Close your eyes and pay attention. I'm going to show you some stretches." "OK", i replied. "You have my undivided attention."

For the next thirty minutes i was instructed in a number of very specific stretches for my entire pelvic region. He showed me an image of a position i assumed it and followed his instructions. He also gave me a timed process which allowed my tissues to respond without forcing them into undue discomfort. My teacher as-

serted that i must give the muscles and other tissues time to adjust to the stretches. This was a whole new approach for me. He wanted me to listen to my tissues – how interesting!

My back loved the way it felt. i had been gifted with a way to treat myself. Since that morning, twenty years ago in the park, my back has not 'gone out' but twice – and that only after a new injury. My body sends me clues when i neglect to stretch for too long. Over the years, i instructed over a hundred clients in these exercises, including chiropractors, with excellent results. Kudos to my instructor.

Oh, by the way, my lesson in the park had one more part to it. He gave me an alternative approach to my in-service with the managerial staff that worked much better than the way i had planned. The program was an immense success. What would i ever do without the 'help of my friends?'

PASS IT ON

It was approaching midnight. It was cold and

beginning to snow while i shivered on the side of the interstate highway outside of Washington, DC.

Five days earlier i left Ft Hood, Texas after learning of the possibility of being sent back to Vietnam with an infantry battalion. i realized that the government was not interested in my welfare, so i left the military without its permission. One of my GI friends drove me to a station where i boarded a bus to Dallas. From there on i was AWOL (absent without leave) and hitchhiking across the US. Come hell or high water, i was not going back to Vietnam.

Armed with a duffle bag full of clothing, a guitar and Joni Mitchell's recording of Clouds, i thumbed my way across to Florida before heading north. i managed to sleep in the vehicles that picked me up or on the side of the roadways. Spring weather along the southern route afforded me the opportunity to sleep outside. Once i headed northward, things changed. By the time i hit the beltway outside of DC that night, it was cold.

71

The through traffic was intermittent and I grew tired and weary.

i wanted to sleep, even if just for an hour or two. i had plenty of clothes i could layer in hopes of staying reasonably warm. As i started going through the duffle bag, a very clear voice spoke inside my head. "If you go to sleep, you will die." i took out another long-sleeved shirt and put it on under my jacket.

Another half hour went by and i only grew colder and colder.

i began jumping up and down, moving my arms and legs in order to pump warm blood. Nothing seemed to help.

i thought, *this is it; i could die here. If i just lay down, nothing will matter.*

The voice came again, "Just stay awake, not long now."

i continued jumping up and down, shaking my limbs and walking around in circles. Minutes

later out of the darkness came a semi.

While the driver slowed to a stop i grabbed my stuff and ran, all the while saying 'thank you, thank you, thank you' – to whom besides the driver, i had no idea.

He asked where i was headed. "Boston," i said. "I'm on my way to New Hampshire," he told me. "I can drop you off on 495 just outside the city." i replied, "That would be great. Thank you very much for stopping. It's getting pretty cold out there."

He asked where I came from and what was i doing out on the highway in the middle of such a cold night? i told him my story. He seemed to understand and said, "Why don't you get some sleep now. I'll wake you in a few hours." Within sixty seconds i went out like a light.

i awoke when i felt the semi slowing down to a stop. Once parked, the driver asked me if i had any money. "Not much," i replied, "$2.37 to be exact."

He said, "Come on in, I'll buy you breakfast." During the meal, he confided in me that he had been in the Korean conflict. He understood why i left the military and would have done the same himself if he thought he had to go back to war.

A couple of hours later, he brought the truck to a stop close to the city of Boston. Before i gathered my gear, he said, "Here, take this" as he handed me a twenty dollar bill. "You'll need it. Good luck." Surprised at his kindness, i replied, "Wow, thank you very much. If you write down your address, i will mail it to you as soon as i can." All he said was "Pass it on. You'll know when."

As i watched him drive away, i felt hopeful that there was still some goodness left in humanity. On that spring morning i walked off the highway, food in my belly and a few bucks in my pocket, in search of a telephone.

Since that experience i have gladly and without hesitation 'passed it on' whenever it was needed. One person can make a difference.

ALL YOU NEED IS LOVE

The year following my release from the military i took an opportunity to cruise the coast north of Portland, Maine. Without time restraints, i had the whole day to myself, happy to have the freedom to move around.

i picked up a hitchhiker on the way out to the ocean. He seemed friendly enough as we chatted about all kinds of topics while driving the country roads. He told me of a small island that could only be accessed at low tide. It sounded interesting, so off we headed. While on the island and he began talking of witch craft and the power of darkness. After a couple minutes, i stated that i had no interest in that kind of stuff. i told him i was leaving and if he wanted a ride back to town, now was the time to go.

On the return drive, something about him changed. Little by little i felt the presence of something in the car which seemed to be coming through my passenger. i felt a chill and a growing sense of threat. This power, or whatever, was attempting to take over my being. It felt

horrible; i became frightened. i sensed a battle was taking place for my very soul and i was losing. i asked from deep within myself for help.

Almost instantly i started receiving images of people whom i loved. One by one they floated onto my mental screen. Each image had a bright light around the person's face. As they continued to flow into my mind, i felt a power grow within me. i somehow knew it was important to continue this gathering of intensity. i gained more control, yet knew i needed something else. At once an inner voice said "Turn on the radio NOW!" i reached out and hit the power button.

The song All You Need is Love by the Beatles came through the speakers. i sang the words with everything that was in me. The battle was over by the time the song ended.

My passenger was shaking violently and wanted out of the car immediately. Before he left i said, "Love is the most powerful force in all the universes." Without looking at me, he jumped out of the vehicle and ran down the street.

A THOUGHT

i could go on and on with questions. How did i know what to do at just the right time? Who was sending me these messages? How can he, she or they synchronize so many things at one time? Is this wisdom part of me?

i have discovered some of these answers for myself as we all must do, but that doesn't matter.

What is of importance is that we receive this guidance and act upon it. The more we partake in this wisdom, the more we come to trust ITS presence in our lives.

CHAPTER SIX

Learning to Let Go

Surrender is perhaps one of the most difficult obstacles to overcome when choosing to live a spiritually oriented lifestyle. Whether a person practices a path of meditation, contemplation or religion, the task of surrender is a constant battle between the human personality (call it ego if you wish) and the spiritual being. Some people use the terms higher and lower self to describe this personal struggle.

Many of us are manifestors. We make things happen. We decide to accomplish some feat

or create a situation, and then make it happen. Throughout much of my life, i have made goals for one, three or five years into the future. Within the allotted time, I materialized those plans and felt pride in doing so. That was part of my forte. i surrounded myself with people of like nature – we were creators.

As i followed the whisperings of intuition more and more over the years (mainly because it worked), i grew less and less self-willed. My trust in inner guidance took over as i let go of my own ideas and opinions and simply listened. i discovered that Life was talking constantly through all of its forms. The messages came from plants, animals, dreams, minerals, other people and my inner guides. When they spoke, i listened and amazing things happened. The minute details and the synchronicity of events are wonders in themselves. This continues to happen to this day.

THE LETTER

Years and years after the break-up of a long term relationship, i continued to hold some re-

sentment and anger towards the other person. It didn't take much to set me off on an emotional tirade.

Every time she pushed one of my buttons over the phone, click, I slammed down the receiver then roamed and ranted around the house. i knew that this behavior was not healthy, but i still carried on as though i had no control over my reactions.

While pulling weeds in the garden one afternoon, the voice came. Clear and concise, it said, "You must write her a letter of forgiveness." i knew exactly who the voice was talking about. "No way," I blurted. "It's not my responsibility to do all the forgiving; i won't do it."

Once the seed was planted, it took me about three days before i consented. By then i decided that a letter wasn't sufficient enough.

If i were to be genuine, then more must be done. i chose to make her a cassette tape of music that we both enjoyed in the past plus some meaningful songs of my own discovering.

It took me about ten hours to complete both the tape and a letter. i put in as much love, respect and honesty as possible. i made a copy of the music before i sent them both off in the mail.

Later on that afternoon as i listened to the tape, i had an epiphany – the whole exercise was solely for my benefit. i realized that i released myself from my very own emotional prison. It was all about my freedom. Knowing that something important just happened, i wrote the following phrase on the cover of the cassette: *Time Released Freedom.*

MY LITTLE GETAWAY

My sweetie was away in Europe visiting with her sons and some friends. i remained at home on the island in charge of the house and dogs.

Being part of a housing complex, there is always something going wrong or needing repair. i stayed pretty busy for the week or so with surfing, gardening, small repairs, writing, editing and caring for the dogs.

After a week, i started thinking that i should treat myself to a mini getaway. i kept getting images and nudges to drive to a small town on the coast and spend one night in a funky little hotel that we have frequented before. The town is very small and somewhat bereft, yet sits on a beautiful bay. The color of the water is mesmerizing as it changes with the movement of the sun throughout the day and into the evening. Each time there, i sit on the porch staring at the mountains dumping into the ocean. i feel a warm sense of peace wash over and through me.

At the thought of enjoying that feeling again, i decided that's where i wanted to go. i deserved a break. i made the arrangements.

On the scheduled day i drove the two and a half hours, checked in and took and short nap. Afterwards i grabbed my laptop and headed for the restaurant, figuring i could ring up my sweetie in Europe and get some work done.

The hotel owner greeted me and, after a few minutes of chatting, asked me if i wanted to

have dinner with a gringo and his wife who were down from the states. They didn't speak Spanish and were hoping to find someone who spoke English. *Great*, I thought. i came here for some peace and quiet and now this guy wants me to be 'social'. Before i could come up with a suitable excuse, i said, "OK, what time?" i couldn't believe i said that; i wanted to be alone. Oh well, there is a reason for everything.

That evening i met the couple.

We shared the usual opening conversation, where are you from and what do you do? They seemed very pleasant and talkative, glad to be with someone who speaks their language.

The meal, as usual in this place, was superb; fresh fish and roasted vegetables. We continued to talk throughout dinner about the things we do in our daily lives. Once the food was done, the man got up and went for a smoke, leaving his wife and i at the table to carry on.

Our conversation turned to more personal is-sues and topics. The woman confessed that

she couldn't find anyone to talk about real life stuff and always felt that she was invisible and strange. At one point, the topic turned to intuition and the world of spiritual matters. She opened right up, speaking of childhood events and experiences that have affected her life to the present day. She began crying and told me she felt that 'someone had finally seen her, really seen her.'

i simply presented her with platforms from which she could draw her own conclusions. By the time her husband returned she had changed quite dramatically. He recognized the transformation and remarked what an incredible woman she had always been for him. He voiced his support of her expressing more of herself in the future.

We wound down the conversation and bid each other warm farewells with promises to keep in touch. The woman hugged me tightly, then looked into my eyes and said 'Thank you'.

i felt the gratitude come from deep within her. It was then i realized that my little getaway was

actually for the benefit of this woman and her husband.

The interesting thing about these kinds of experiences is that i become fuller and more whole as a person whenever i accept the role of a channel for another soul. How spirit sets up such events down to the minute details, is totally beyond my scope of understanding. i am forever amazed.

LOCKED IN THE CLOSET

The ten year relationship was coming to an end although neither of us really wanted to admit it. i had recently awakened from a period of spiritual slumber and struggled with my present life situation. i was torn between continuing with a dying relationship (therefore going back to sleep) and not wanting to fail and/or hurt my partner. There seemed no positive way out of the situation.

For a few weeks i kept getting this nudge to lock myself in a closet. i thought, hey, *that's not a bad idea; I could block out any outside stimuli and*

deterrents to my being focused. That way i could hear myself think and maybe come up with an answer to my dilemma. Then i caught myself. *That's insane, what would people think? What's the matter with you?*

Day after day, the thought of spending some time in the closet alone entered my consciousness along with that little voice, "yes that is a good idea." Finally i gave in.

One weekend afternoon i approached my partner and told her of my plan. i said to her, "i need some answers to things that i am confused about. Follow me. This is gonna sound nuts, but i'm going to lock myself in this closet and under no circumstances do i want to be disturbed. i may be in there for quite a while, but do not open this door. Please believe that i know what i'm doing."

In that two by four foot closet i remained for three hours and twenty minutes until i had what i sought. My answers were very clear. No matter what happened with the relationship, i knew that i must first, and foremost, follow my

spiritual path. It felt so good to be awake again. i knew that i would never lose that feeling again, no matter what came my way.

Of course, my partner thought i was a bit whacked in the head. i heard her on the phone in another room a few days later telling a friend that i locked myself in the closet. During our relationship she often thought of my spiritual experiences as 'off the wall'. She called them 'Woo-Woo' stuff. Guess i was finished defending my way of life. i have never turned back.

A TEST

There are many times when in a public setting, i receive little whispers to 'turn this way' or 'walk over there'. A real common one is 'pay attention now'. These nudges are sometimes accompanied with a slight ringing in my ears or some other sound that i have become accustomed to hearing. Then something happens. An infant may be beaming me or someone will catch my attention, followed by a kind of inner transference like energy passing between us.

There are times when a full blown conversation happens that was 'just what that person needed at that particular time in their life.'

Whether subtle or dramatic i am usually left aware of the reason for the message. This, however, is not always the case.

A Halloween party was scheduled that night at an art gallery in a small town in New Mexico. Typically i don't like Halloween, or parties for that matter, but earlier in the afternoon i received a strong sense that i must go to this gathering.

An hour prior to leaving i talked with my friend, Roger, about attending the event. He had no interest whatsoever in going. i voiced some doubts about making the effort, especially when i am not particularly fond of such parties.

He asked me, "Why would you go to something if you don't really want to?" i replied, "i'm not sure. Something tells me i need to go." He quipped, "Do you always do things that you don't want to? Who is telling you to do this?"

89

"My inner voice tells me that i need to be there. For whatever reason, i don't have a clue. i will let you know when i come back."

i walked the few blocks to the art gallery. Outside of making eye contact with a few people and some short conversations, nothing really happened. The art work was delightful and entertaining. An hour into the event, the little voice made itself known. "You can leave now," was all it said. i scanned the rooms to check if anything or anyone came up on last minute radar. Nope. Nothing – i left.

On the corner across the street i noticed a park bench. i walked over and sat down, wondering what this experience was all about. i could not discern any reason as to why i had to be present at this particular event. Then the tiniest little whisper of a voice said, "You don't have to know. You just have to surrender and follow." That was it in a nutshell.

Who knows why we are placed in situations that have no apparent justification? Maybe it is simply an eye contact, a kind word or vibrating

at a certain frequency that is needed in a situation. The important issue is that we listen to and follow our inner guidance, period.

With these thoughts rolling around in my head, i ambled back to Roger's house. We sat down and i reported the evening's events and my conclusion.

Once i finished he smiled and said, "You know, you're right; we really don't have to know the whys. We just have to listen and trust."

TRUST THE PROCESS

During the therapist retreat we split off into groups of three and entered the water. Two of us treated while the third received a treatment. i was the lead therapist for the session. The therapist/client lay back in the warm water.

Within a matter of a few minutes she moved out into the main body of the lagoon as we held onto her. Her body began to unwind and release some of its tension. Without planning or thinking i received a nudge to go under the water

beneath her and lift her onto my shoulder. As i did so, she rolled over onto her stomach which put her into a fireman type carry over my shoulder. The voice said, "Run as fast as you can." So i did. i ran for approximately fifty yards dragging her through the water.

When i stopped, she was coughing and gagging from swallowing water. Once she calmed i asked if she was OK. She said "Yes, I'm fine. Do it again." I rolled her back onto my shoulder and took off while her head dragged in the water.

Again the voice said, "Stop here." The woman coughed up more water than the first time.

The other therapist was eyeing me as though i was completely insane. i thought the woman might possibly drown but knew somehow that this was the right thing to do. The client regained her composure and repeated, "Do it again, one more time." "Alright," i said and ran through the water with her head and shoulders trailing behind under the surface.

This time we stopped, she rolled over and curled up into my arms in a fetal position. Her hands and feet were pressed closely together. She went completely still and quiet for a moment or two.

Suddenly her closed eyelids began to flutter; her body started to heave with uncontrollable sobs. i softly whispered into her ear, "Can you tell me what is happening?" She described herself as a young girl bound at her hands and feet and being carried on the shoulder of a man as he ran. Then she was thrown on the ground. From there, she witnessed her family being killed. Then she wept as she sank deep into my arms.

We held her between us as she went through her experience and process.

About fifteen minutes later she began to verbalize and question why this happened to her family. Suddenly her facial expression changed. She spoke out saying, "Oh my God, it is the Archangel, Gabriel. He's here." i encouraged her to ask him about her experience and what it meant.

Again she went silent although this time her body grew peaceful and relaxed. Occasionally her eyes filled with tears but her face held an expression of joy.

Once she finished and was able to integrate the experience within her body, we ended the session. Later on in the day she related her experience and how it tied directly into her present day life including her son and family members. She also reported that her belief in past lives and angels had come to life.

She pulled me aside a bit later to personally thank me for listening to my intuition and following her desire to be dragged through the water even though it seemed inappropriate and unconventional at the time.

i expressed my gratitude for her trust and the opportunity to partake in such a special experience. i also told her that it was her inner guidance and wisdom that guided us all through the event. She was the courageous one.

Experiences such as these help us learn to surren-

der to inner wisdom. Beyond rational thought and socially accepted belief systems, this way of living and learning far surpasses anything else i have discovered. Intuition proves itself to me again and again when reason has fallen short. Surrender is never easy on the ego for we tend to believe that we are the end all when it comes to intelligence and wisdom. Where ever did we get that belief in the first place?

CHAPTER SEVEN

When You Don't Want to Hear It

How many times have you heard that little voice inside tell you to do a particular thing that you really did not want to do? This had happened to me numerous times. Going along, minding my own business and out of the blue a message comes through, soft but firm, "You must do.............." My first reaction is typically, "No, i don't want to; are you crazy? Go away."

Occasionally, it will go away, but more likely than not, the guidance is persistent, especially

when it is good for my freedom and / or growth. Looking back on these experiences, i must laugh. My childish ego only wants to do what i decide or chose to engage in. Until i let go of this attitude and its inherent temper tantrums, i waste time carrying on like a two year old. Over the years i've shown improvement with my re-action time, making it much easier to accept these amazing pieces of guidance.

Letting go of the past, or doing things against our comfort zones, requires change. Change is not easy, especially if it causes discomfort or compromises our beliefs. Many of us, me in-cluded, welcome change if we believe that it will make our lives more pleasant or rewarding. However, introduce change that promises hard-ship, fear or reorganization of our basic belief systems and we sing a different tune.

My entire life has been riddled with consistent changes, many of them huge. No matter how i reacted or accepted these alterations to my life, they just keep coming. In fact, if nothing chang-es in my environment for a couple of months, i grow anxious and wonder what is wrong.

Each of the following experiences taught me something greater about myself and the world around me. Some of these events have radically changed the way i view myself.

Without them, my life would be different – i would be different.

FACING A LIFE LONG FEAR

Ever since i started surfing, the fear of sharks has rattled my cage. At eighteen years old, i experienced a past lifetime when a shark bit my leg off at the knee and i bled to death. No matter what body of water i found myself in (lake, ocean or pool), the fear was present. i saw sharks at Florida surf spots; even ran over a couple with my surfboard. The fear was always there, yet my love for surfing was greater.

i accepted a job offer on the island of Oahu despite the 75% cut in pay. In my mid-forties, i was determined to ride bigger waves of the North shore before i died. i mailed twenty boxes of stuff that i might need and jumped on a plane.

Over the next few months, i learned a plethora of information about the ocean, especially sharks. For instance, the green sea turtle was on the endangered species list, making it illegal for locals to hunt them. They made a great comeback in numbers. Good for turtles and great for tiger sharks as the green turtle is one of its favorite delicacies. Not good for surfers.

Have you ever seen what a person on a surfboard or boogie board looks like from under that water? Yup, dinner.

i frequented breaks by the name of Chun's, Jocko's, Alii beach, Ehukai, Alligator's and Lani's. One of my favorites was Jocko's, a goofy footer's dream when it worked. Every now and then, there was a shark scare; someone would spot one of the large predators and we all grew anxious. One evening, a young local went missing – his boogie board was found the next morning on a beach with his keys on the leash and large teeth marks in the board. He was never found.

Within a month a large tiger shark surfaced at

Chun's and bit off the nose of a surfer's board. We saw the guy later that night on the evening news reporting what happened. A number of people started calling the tiger, the 'Bart Simpson' shark because its dorsal fin was cut and ragged like the cartoon figure's hair. We were all freaked out. Nobody went in the water alone; everyone grouped tightly together at the local breaks.

A few weeks passed, a local surfer/fisherman caught the shark. The tiger measured 14.5 feet long. My cousin wanted me to nail the dorsal fin to a telephone pole at Chun's reef. i flatly refused, fearing that I might enrage the shark God. A friend of my cousin's cured the jaws in salt. He encouraged me to hold the bone and step inside the jaws comprised of rows of razor sharp teeth. i got the 'willys' while noticing how large the mouth was and how easily i fit inside of them.

i didn't sleep well at all for the next few nights, my dreams filled with sharks.

Following the capture of Bart Simpson, most of

the people in the water remained alert and cautious. You could feel the fear hanging in the air, especially at Chun's. i was petrified every time i went out.

One of my hospital clients, a local diver, gave me some tips about living with sharks.

He reminded me that when the turtles are near, or on the surface, all is fine. If they disappear or dive quickly, it is time to pay attention.

Number two: sharks are wild predators – when you feel that natural instinct you are being hunted (a buzz up your spine) – leave the water. And number three: sharks hunt mostly at night, so when the sun is approximately one inch from sinking into the horizon, it is time to take yourself 'off the menu.' i started paying attention to these cues and felt 1/100th better, yet still spooked.

My cousin and i arrived at Chun's/Jocko's for the dawn patrol session (the breaks are separated by a small inlet a quarter of a mile wide). Jocko's was my all-time favorite break.

Both breaks looked epic, however, there were a dozen people out at Chun's and no one surfing Jocko's. My cousin paddled out while i remained on the beach staring at Jocko's. Suddenly, i heard a voice behind me, "I'll go out if you will."

i knew it was time to face the fear. "Let's go," i said.

My skin tingling from panic, i paddled out to the break and had the session of my life. i danced on the water, completely melded with the waves.

About thirty minutes into the session, the other guy's leash broke. He swam into shore leaving me completely alone and spooked to the max.

i turned seaward and screamed, "Ok, Mano (the Hawaiian name for shark), i can't do this anymore. If you want me, come get me." i was out of my mind with fear and i wanted it to end.

i rode a few more waves before reasoning kicked in.

There i sat, out in the ocean, by myself, knowing full well that i could be eaten at any moment. That was enough for me. i proved to myself that i could face my fear. i started the quarter of a mile paddle over to Chun's to hook up with my cousin. i felt proud of myself.

Suddenly, about eight feet in front of me a fin emerged from the water.

i went into total fright as did my bladder. It took another whole second or so to realize that the fin was actually the flipper of a green sea turtle. i burst into uncontrollable laughter. Yup, i controlled that fear, alright. My cousin chuckled for days.

Sometimes fear can keep us alive. Abnormal fears, however, can cripple us from doing some of the things we love. Many times the fear is greater than the actual event or memory of the experience.

Intuition can help by using our own natural instincts and the wisdom of others in order to live with those fears.

YOU WILL FAST

It was my birthday. i crawled out of my tent ready for a day of biking around the desert of south central Utah with Ralph, my dog.

While having my second cup of coffee a visitor showed up. This was not your regular type of visitor but one of my cherished inner guides. Without fanfare he told me that i was to 'fast for forty days'. Now, i have fasted in the past quite a bit (once a week for a day or a three day fast now and then, ten days being my longest). But i definitely did not want to fast for that long. So, of course, i said "No."

i cleaned and packed my dishes and hit the trails. The morning gleamed with bright sun, blue skies and red rock walls towering over the desert floor in mesas and pistol butte formations.

Ralph and i cruised for miles stopping whenever we felt like it. Throughout the day, my visitor appeared and repeated the same message, "You will fast for 40 days." Each time i replied with

"No, no way."

Late afternoon came and slid into early evening.

i finished dinner, lit a fire and settled in to write the annual evaluation of my life, something i have done every year on my birth date for some twenty odd years. Directly across the fire pit, my visitor appeared. With coal, black eyes prodding deep inside me, he repeated, "You WILL fast for forty days." This was not merely a statement; it was a command.

"OK," i said. "You want me to die, then i'll die. You want me to die a slow and painful death? Alright then, i'll die. Fine, i'll go ahead and die." i finished writing my evaluation and sat by the fire thinking about what i had agreed to.

As the fire dimmed and the stars lit up the canyon, i began to wonder if i had truly lost my mind. How was i going to undertake such a monumental task and work at the same time? Didn't i need to find a cave and disappear from humanity so i could emerge as an enlightened

being? i awoke somewhere around 3 or 4 am to the brilliance of the Milky Way and crawled into the tent.

For the first ten days i drank only water with pure lemon juice, maple syrup and cayenne pepper (12 tablespoons of lemon and syrup and 1/2 teaspoon pepper to 1 gallon of water). Oh, and don't forget the coffee. Every fast deserves coffee. i had done this particular fast before, so i knew what to expect. Once these ten days passed, i felt physically clean and strong, almost super human.

From then on, my only meal was freshly juiced veggies once a day.

Many purists say that this is not a real fast, and i agree, however, this was MY fast and i decided what kind it would be. The first ten days cleaned out the physical body – the second ten days purified my emotional body. i found myself crying from the fact that i couldn't reward myself with food. *Ahhh*! The smell of pizza set me off. All my emotions became heightened. i felt charged both physically and emotionally.

Towards the twenty day mark, i started to experience an emotional purity that i had never before known.

My friends and people at work watched me carefully, expecting me to crash at any moment. Little did they know that i grew stronger and more resolved as each day passed. On the 22nd day, one of the secretaries, who had voiced a growing concern about my health, brought me a piece of chocolate cake and a glass of milk. She said, "You must eat something before you die." i informed her, "if i eat that cake, i just might die."

Two days later she told me, "For someone who hasn't eaten for so long, you look really good." She simply couldn't believe it.

The third ten day stretch worked on my mental status. i continued to go out with people to restaurants – i ordered either herbal tea or hot water with lemon. The sight of people eating became offensive to me; the very thought of spending so much time and energy preparing food seemed a waste. As i approached thirty

days, something i had not expected began to happen. i started seeing auras and energy fields around people, situations and objects. Finally, i understood why my inner guide wanted me to fast for so long. i became privy to the Life Source that surrounded and permeated everything. i felt connected with the Essence of Life itself. i loved it. i never wanted to eat solid food again.

In this state of consciousness, i drove a day and a half to attend a major seminar on spirituality. My next observable change (to me, anyway) became apparent. i entered a profound state of humility as i attended the workshops and programs. i felt filled with a pure essence that i knew was present in all living and non-organic objects. And to top it off, i was part of it all. THIS is what my guide wanted for me.

On the ride back to Utah, i realized that i completed my agreement with my 'visitor.'

i knew it was time to join the world of eating again. What started out as a seemingly impossible task ended as one of the most remarkable

experiences of my life. i shall be forever grateful to that great Soul who gave me a push in a direction i never would've attempted by myself.

NOT SUCH A NICE GUY

If we accept the concept of karma and reincarnation, it is plausible that we may have lived hundreds or thousands of lifetimes.

That is a lot of opportunities to get into some pretty serious mischief. We all like to believe that we have lived as benevolent kings, queens, saviors or other honorable individuals. History, however, has proven this not to be true. As a species we have behaved horribly towards each other – killing, torturing, stealing, abusing, conniving and a myriad of other awful behaviors (the Inquisitions, brutalities, hundreds of wars and genocides).

One simply has to look at the lack of ethics in today's business or political environments to understand that the name of the game is 'money and power.'

110

This is not to say that these are the only ways we have acted in the past. Of course, there are many times when we have been kind, loving, caring and otherwise helpful and serving human beings. After all, this world seems to be a school ground for us to learn how to love as opposed to amassing power and control. We all go through this process.

There seems no escape from it.

i've had my share of experiences where i saw some of my darker moments. They disturbed me greatly every single time. Perhaps the most unsettling event was the realization that i tortured others in another lifetime. i don't know what time period this took place but it was very clear that i used some horrible implements and methods to inflict terrible pain and death. Guilt and shame of this knowledge tore at my heart for weeks on end. How could i have done such cruel things to others?

Following this experience, i witnessed other past life events where i was the one being tortured. i saw and understood that the scales of

karma must be balanced, therefore, i had to pay in exact measure. i learned about the abuse of power from both sides of the fence. i believe that these experiences are the causes of why i spent so much of this lifetime in the field of human service.

i knew right from the beginning of my career that, first and foremost, i must act out of love and kindness to all with whom i came in contact. It could never be 'about the money' or 'professional expertise'; it had to be about love. This has been the driving element underlying my professional and personal life.

For certain, i did not want this kind of information. Knowledge and experience of these events from my past, no matter how difficult they were to witness, have affected my life in a profound manner. Without them, would i be the person that i have become today? i really don't think so. As hard as it can be, that is the nature of change and growth.

CHAPTER EIGHT

Exercises to Build Your Intuitive Power

If we want stronger muscles we exercise. To have a better vocabulary we read. If we want to play an instrument we take the time to learn. The same holds true with building our intuitive skills; we must practice. The great thing about practicing intuitive skills is that you can exercise them anywhere and everywhere.

You can't take a gym with you, but your sensations go where you go. As with all skills, the

more you practice, the better they get. The following pages contain activities and exercises i encourage you to put to use.

You may notice immediate improvements with some and slower, more gradual progress with others. Try them all and keep what works. Don't forget to pass them on to others. The more we are aware, the better it is for all of us.

LISTENING TO YOUR WORLD

Each of us lives in slightly (or radically) different worlds from deserts to mountains, by the oceans, interior plains or ice caps.

Many of us dwell within cities, others in rural areas. No matter where we live our environments are filled with species of all sorts including other people, animals, mammals, birds, plants, minerals, etc.

If we accept the basic principle that all life forms have consciousness, then it is not that much of a stretch to believe that all forms of life are communicating in one way or another. It is the in-

tent of this chapter to invite and encourage you to listen and pay attention to the life forms that surround you.

For example, when you encounter a dog or a cat, a bird or a cow; say, "Hi" (silently if you wish not to embarrass yourself). When you greet them, speak in a natural voice much the same way you would use in salutation to another person. In other words, treat them as an equal. Like a young child, they know when you are genuine. i am always amused when i watch someone approach a grown dog as though they were greeting an infant. i often wonder what the dog thinks about that. The same principal goes for plants. Let the plant know that you are sincere.

In the beginning ask the being what it is saying to you. You may want to ask a dog, for example, "What are you saying to me?" Invent your own phrases. For a while this may help you tune in to the beings you are addressing. After a bit of practice you won't need this; you will automatically think it and the being will know. i've made it a habit to say *hi* to everything and anything.

While walking through my gardens each day i greet many of the plants with "Hi there," or "You look beautiful," or "Is there anything you need for me to do?"

Train yourself to notice anything unusual or out of the ordinary. Does an animal want to approach you but is weary of something? Does a wild bird fly particularly close to you or seem to follow you?

Does a co-worker seem preoccupied or sad? These are all clues that you will pick up if you pay attention.

Try to establish the attitude that all life is talking all the time.

PLAY YOUR HUNCHES

Whenever you get a nudge or hear a voice within yourself telling you to do something, consider it as a message that is meant only for you. It may be instructing you in something as simple as "Take your umbrella with you today" or "Call so and so." On the other hand, it could be

a major piece of wisdom such as "Do not take that job." If the information feels right, act upon it. If it seems 'way out there', let it go.

Many individuals use the '3 times' technique. That is, if you get a message, image or hunch three times, then you know it is okay to act on it. NEVER act upon a message that tells you to harm another person or do something that you know is wrong.

It may, however, involve something that is uncomfortable like telling someone that you don't want to continue with a relationship.

You will know instinctively that inner guidance is leading you in the right direction even if it is a difficult task. Once you start paying attention and trying out a few hunches, you will enter a learning curve and begin to see what works and what doesn't, what is realistic and on target and what is absurd.

Other people utilize a 'yes-no' or 'green light-red light' tool. Once they receive a message, they envision a yes sign on one side of their

mental screen and a no sign on the other side (or red light-green light). Whichever sign lights up, that is their answer.

THE TRUTH METER

This particular tool or method is very useful in reading other people. i cannot for the life of me remember where i came across this technique. It might have been from somewhere in the therapeutic world where i spent many, many years of practice.

May have come from my spiritual background or, it might have just popped up out of the ethers. It would be helpful to know so i could give credit where it is due. Either way, here it is.

When another person says something to you, try to imagine where you feel that within your own body. For example, if i told you that i owned a six-legged cat, you know that is false: but where do you feel that? Do you sense that in your stomach, knee, throat, head or your little toe? Now, if i told you that this book is about intuition, how different would that feel? Notice

the difference in feelings between the two statements and where it settles in your body.

You can practice this technique with a relative or a friend. Tell each other obvious truths and lies at first. Then use less obvious statements and watch what happens.

Once you become conscious of where these sensations happen in your body and can discriminate between truths and falsehoods, you can put this method into general practice. Many individuals find this a very helpful tool in their daily interactions with others. A side benefit is an increased awareness of our own body parts.

In my therapeutic background, i learned to listen to the body wisdom of my clients. Many of the alternative therapies encourage clients to begin communicating with their body parts.

If you are experiencing difficulty or pain somewhere in your body, try holding a conversation with that body part. Ask what it needs or what the discomfort is trying to teach you. Why do you need this particular experience? Is your

body trying to tell you something? You can do this with any body part, even your cells. Give it a whirl; what do you have to lose?

WHICH WAY DO I GO?

Washington, DC in the springtime can be beautiful when the cherry trees are in blossom. i visited the capitol for a spiritual seminar.

i think the year was sometime in the mid nineties (so much for an accurate memory – my life has been so full that dates often elude me). Anyhow, the seminar was intense for me. At one point i needed to go outside and walk for a while. Maybe walking would help me integrate the hundreds of things that were flying through my mind.

Once outside the hotel, standing on the sidewalk, i couldn't decide which way to go. i stood there for quite a few minutes unable to make up my mind. Suddenly, yup, you guessed it, the little voice. The whisper said, "Why don't you ask?" "OK," i said, "Which way do I go?" "Left," i heard. i walked down the city block and when

i reached the next street, i asked again. Promptly i was informed.

Every time i walked the length of a block i inquired as to which way to turn. Each time i received an immediate answer. At one particular cross street, instead of being told where to turn, i was instructed to 'look all around and notice what comes to your attention.'

Sure enough, within thirty seconds i saw something that struck my attention. That something held a direct meaning for me. As soon as i understood, the whisper told me which way to go.

This little adventure went on for two and a half hours. i finally ended up at some formal building with unique statues, the like i've never seen before. Somehow i knew that this was a place to sit for a while. After pondering what i had just experienced, i realized that i was given an exercise in both surrender and building my intuitive skill of listening to inner wisdom. When i returned to the hotel, using the same technique, i felt centered and assured, my mind calm.

Since that city experience i have taught this technique to many other individuals. Some of my favorite settings to hold this exercise are in wooded areas next to the ocean or a lake. i advise the participants to begin with the statement, "Which way do I turn?" This is followed by "Every time you begin to think, stop. Ask again, which way do I turn?"

Ask, walk, think, stop, ask, and walk as simple as that. i encourage them to notice any wildlife, plants, rocks or other objects that capture their attention. Take a moment to realize what that particular object has to say, then ask, "Which way do I go?"

i typically give the group of participants 30-45 minutes to complete their walk before returning to a central meeting place for a discussion and sharing period. The stories are very interesting. Most people discover that they inherently possessed the skill and realize how easily they could tune into it.

You can perform this exercise as a walk, a bike ride or cruising around in your car. Again, the

central behavior is 'paying attention' to what is coming from within you and your surroundings.

DREAMS

Both day and night dreams are jammed packed with wisdom and guidance. Train yourself to remember your dreams. If this is difficult for you, try saying to yourself, "I will remember my dreams upon awakening" ten times right before you fall off to sleep. This should help bring them to your awareness. Keep a notebook and a writing utensil next to your bed. Make it a habit to write down something about the dream even if it is just a feeling that stays with you upon awakening. If you really want to glean as much information from your dreams as possible, read your dream journal once a week or once a month.

You may notice how much your dream life relates to your waking existence.

There are many books on dreaming and dream interpretation, however, trust your own mean-

ings. Granted, there are some symbols that have generalized meanings for many, but overall, you are a unique individual with your own dream experiences exclusively meant for you.

AN INNER GUIDE

Once you delve into the worlds of intuition and inner guidance, you may naturally evolve to the state where you begin to seek a spiritual guide. If you presently have such a helper in your life, build your relationship with him/her. You may have one and not be aware of it. For example, do you have a spiritual figure in your religion that you trust? If so, start asking that being for guidance in simple ways. Start having daily conversations with your guide or savior.

If you don't have an inner guide, try this exercise. Sit in a quiet place where you won't be disturbed for 30 minutes or so. Get comfortable and close your eyes. Remember a favorite place you frequent in order to think or get away. Go there. Envision your surroundings including sights, sounds, smells, weather and anything else that plays on your mental screen.

124

Once you have relaxed into your spot, ask out loud, "Is there anyone here who could be my guide?" Use whatever phrase comes to your mind in the asking. Wait and watch. When someone shows up, ask him or her if they are here for your benefit as a spiritual guide. If nothing happens the first time, try at some other time. When a true guide appears, you should feel filled with the rightness of his/her presence.

Another way to find a spiritual guide is simply to ask for one to appear in your dreams. Watch for signs both inside and outside. You may be surprised at what comes your way. You could possibly realize that you have more than one or many guides. There is an ancient saying that "When the student is ready, a master will appear."

Many guides operate only within the invisible worlds but that does not diminish their ability to send us help via intuition or inner wisdom.

The ideal, of course, is to find a spiritual guide who can operate both on the inner and within the physical world.

Hopefully some of these activities and exercises will be helpful in building your intuitive skills. If you already experience and use intuition as a living practice, these may further sharpen your skills. As is true with most spiritual tools, you may discover many techniques of your own that fit you perfectly.

Remember, we are constantly growing and evolving, so what works one day may not work down the road. We are all creating our ways home. There is no end to this process.

CHAPTER NINE

Planning Your Future

There are many possible directions we can take in life. How is it that we come to decide where we live, what job we do or with whom we share a relationship? For a number of people, these are tough choices which take a great amount of mental energy.

We have all, at one time or another, used the 'go – no go or pro & con' lists of decision making process.

This makes us reason out a solution and can be

quite helpful at times. However, our perceptions at that particular time color and direct our decisions. What would happen if we set up a general blueprint of our goal and then let inner guidance fill in the details?

The following experiences were formed in just that manner where i depended upon intuition to fill in the gaps and the how's. To be honest, once i start this process, i usually have no idea how it will take place or where it will lead me.

A LESSON IN OMAHA

A few weeks after i gave an extended treatment session to a Reiki Master, she called me on the telephone. She wanted to know if i would consider flying to Omaha, Nebraska for a weekend in order to treat a number of people. She would set up the clientele and provide me with meals and hotel accommodations. i told her that i would consider it and get back to her within a few days.

That same night i dreamt of flying to Omaha to do some therapy treatments. i was informed

128

that it was important for me to go there. i awakened early in the morning speaking to no one
in particular, "OK, i'll go. Yes, i will go if that is
what you want of me."

i called the woman to tell her. She asked me
how much i charged for a one hour treatment
session. i opened my mouth to speak and found
myself saying, "i will do it for nothing other
than room and board. i don't know why, but
that is what i am guided to do."

i couldn't believe the words that were coming
out of my mouth as i thought, *what on earth are
you saying? You're giving up a whole weekend to
fly to a city to work for nothing. Are you crazy or
something?* We set the dates. She would send me
the airline tickets. We ended the conversation.

i went through my day in disbelief of what i
agreed to. *What came over me?*

Inner wisdom did not seem so wise to me at the
moment. That night i sat down for a short contemplation. i reminded myself that inner guidance was never wrong and i had to let go and

trust that everything happens for a reason. i put the subject to rest and went to bed.

The Friday came; i drove to the airport in Salt Lake City and boarded the flight to Omaha. Never before had i entertained the idea of visiting this city. i met the Reiki Master and her friend at the baggage claim.

i grabbed my bag and off we went. They drove me to a restaurant where we ate dinner and discussed the schedule for the weekend. They had set up ten back to back sessions for Saturday and six on Sunday morning. i was booked solid. After dinner they deposited me at the hotel informing me of the time to be ready in the morning. As i lay on the bed, i began wondering what i had gotten myself into.

Right on schedule, i was retrieved, taken to breakfast and driven to the place where i would spend the rest of the day. The first client entered the room. Following a brief history and discussion of present issues, we began the session. The client presented a powerful reaction to the treatment. She thanked me profusely before she

left. She also placed a generous tip on the small table by the door. i was a little shocked as i have never received a tip for this kind of work.

The next client appeared. There was very little time for a case history so we just began. This was another strong and positive treatment. Again, i received a grateful thank you (and another tip). What was unfolding here?

By the time the sixth or seventh person came into the room, it was 'straight on the table' – no time for anything other than introductions. Somehow i tuned right into each person's issues.

It was effortless and yet, right on the money for each client. i was running on automatic. Whenever i grew tired, i felt another surge of energy bubbling up from inside. My evaluation and treatment modalities seemed to be specifically geared towards the greatest need of each client. It was as though they were teaching me how to immediately assess and listen to them intuitively.

Sunday morning went the same way. My intuitive skills were accurate and sharpened.

i spent time with six more clients one right after the other. Before i caught my breath i was on the plane to Salt Lake. i didn't feel the least bit tired. On the contrary, i felt energized. i realized that i received a lesson in using intuition. When my mind couldn't keep up with the pace, intuition took over. Instead of thinking about what to do next, i automatically knew by listening to clues from the clients and their bodies.

i understood why i needed to go to Omaha. It was an invitation to a training session for me. The people i treated were also treating me to learn another way of being a better, more efficient therapist. Not only did i gain professionally, i returned home with a bunch of cash in my pocket from all the tips. Nothing is ever wasted when we listen to inner wisdom.

A ROUNDABOUT WAY

Once I learned that i was to move back to the state of Maine, i flew out there to look at some

properties for sale along the mid coast area. i contacted a realtor's office and made an appointment with one of the representatives. i informed the woman what we were looking for: approximately 10 acres or more in a rural setting with water, a livable home and space to expand or build something new. All of this had to be within our price range, of course. She stated that she could show me some properties fitting my description.

We met at the realtor's office. The representative was an older woman who told us that her husband was coming along to provide navigation services. They were an older couple who recently relocated to Maine from New York City. At first, they were cute in the way they disagreed about which way to turn en route to the first property.

After an hour or so of consistently getting lost, they didn't simply disagree, they began to argue with each other. They got downright nasty about it. Eventually we found the property: 80 acres, on a steep hillside, no water and five times the asking price we were looking for. "Don't

worry," the woman said, "we have more places to show you. We'll find you the perfect place."

For the better part of the day, the couple kept arguing, getting lost and presenting us with properties that were either way out of our financial range or run down, dilapidated shacks that were about to crash with the next snowfall.

It didn't matter that i kept repeating our desired property wants; they were on a mission to sell us something – anything.

Just about the time i was ready to scream, the woman stated, "We have one more property to show you."

After getting lost one more time, we found another piece that was completely unrealistic for our needs. We met another realtor at the house site. She couldn't find the owners in order to show us the house. There was something about the young woman that captured my attention. As the older couple herded us toward their car, something whispered in my ear, "Get her business card, now." i excused myself for a moment

and walked over to the woman to ask for her card. "i'll call you tomorrow," i told her.

The navigator and his wife managed to return us to our car without getting lost for the first time that day.

i had a positive feeling that the young realtor would find us a suitable place in the near future. The next day i called her, explained our situation and told her what we were looking for. i informed her that we had to leave later that day but would return in about six months.

"Could you do some research over the next few months and send me a few listings in the mail?" She replied, "I would be glad to do that; I think I have an idea what you are looking for."

We returned to Salt Lake City. i put my house on the market and went about the business of daily life. Three months later, i received a letter from the young realtor that held a half a dozen listing pages. When i opened the envelope and held the listings in my hand, one of them started shaking and exhibited a perceptible aura

around its edges. i singled it out and began to read the details. The piece of paper vibrated in my hand as though it were alive. It had everything i wanted right down to the price. i called the realtor and told her that we would relocate to Maine as soon as my house in Salt Lake sold. i promised to call when we arrived.

Finally, a few months later, my home sold.

Before making the move to Maine, we traveled to Bolivia and Peru including the trek to Machu Picchu. With our vibratory rates adjusted from the journey, we landed in the Northeast ready to begin a new life.

i contacted the realtor and set up an appointment. Once in her office i produced the listing that shook in my hand. It took her a few moments before she stated, "I'm sorry, I cannot find this listing anywhere in our books." i was stunned. "Ask her to look again," the whisper said. So i did.

Twenty minutes later, she returned shaking her head. "I don't know how this happened, but for

some reason, this property listing disappeared within our main system and ended up in some obscure little program.

No one ever looked at the property since it was listed six months ago. In fact, the owner called in last week, worried that no one was interested in it, so she dropped the price another $6,000." All i could manage was a big smile.

That day we walked the entire 58 acres of woods and water. The following day, i put down a deposit and signed the agreement to purchase the land and house.

It was amazing how many things had to 'fall into place' in order for us to be led to this particular property. There are many more instances when i felt guided to do something that took me to the next step in completing a task or an experience. The next event is yet another in a long list of happenings.

FINDING WATER

Within two years after moving in, a local real-

tor approached me stating that 2 ½ acres of land abutting our property had just come up for sale. "Was i interested?" she asked. "Of course, let's talk," i responded. The price was right, inner guidance shouted, "YES," and within 45 days, i owned more of the earth.

While walking my new turf one day, soon after signing the papers, a voice entered my consciousness. "This is where you will build *your transformational center*." As simply as that, a whole new chapter to my life had begun.

A multitude of projects, besides full-time employment, filled my waking and dreaming hours. i needed a well so i called a local drilling company. They would be happy to drill and install a well for me. The man told me that all i had to do was decide where i wanted the well to be drilled. We set a date.

i consulted with the locals about drill sites and heard some pretty scary stories. One man needed three sites drilled before finding water.

Another person ran out of money before he

struck a source. Some people told me that it was a good idea to hire a diviner or geologist to help me. i had absolutely no idea how to proceed.

One morning i walked over to where i thought the building site would be. i spoke out loud. "If i am to build this place, i need a water supply. i don't know what to do. i need help." As though inner wisdom was waiting for me to ask, i heard, "Just go look, walk around and trust your senses."

i began wandering around the yard with my hands out and turned down toward the ground. i felt, a bit foolish at first but then i got a nudge to fill my thoughts with images of water, lots and lots of water.

About fifteen minutes later i found myself standing in one particular spot, my hands buzzing like no tomorrow. i asked, "Is this the place for the well?"

A vertical stream of water gushed onto my mental screen. "i'll take that as a yes." i stuck a stick in the ground and went on with my day.

The next day while clearing brush i found an old, stainless steel faucet lying on the ground.

i picked it up and placed it on the future well site. i chuckled to myself thinking, *what an appropriate marker for my new well.*

On the scheduled day, the men appeared with their big drill truck ready to go to work. "Where is the site?" i pointed to the area and said, "You'll find a faucet right over there. That's the spot." He shot me a quizzical look before starting. From the garden i heard him and his co-orker chuckling when they found my faucet.

By the end of the day, i was the proud owner of a gushing new well. The men remarked at the extraordinary amount of water pressure they had tapped into and asked how i found the site. i told them about my experience. They looked at each other and laughed.

To this day, that antique stainless steel faucet sits atop the well cover as a reminder to trust the guidance of inner wisdom.

AN ITALIAN ADVENTURE

Ah, a trip to romantic Italy – what would i want to see, where would i want to go? i broke out the maps and started planning. Rome was a must, so was the Leaning Tower of Pisa and Tuscany in general. Then i looked a little closer at the map. i saw Assisi and immediately thought of St. Francis and what an important figure he was to me in my young Catholic days. i knew immediately i wanted to visit the place where he received the stigmata.

Ironically, about this same time someone told me of Padre Pio, a Catholic monk who, in the past, displayed extraordinary healing powers. Being a therapist for so long, i must check this guy out.

Then i noticed a place called Metaponto in the boot heel area of the country. It had a picture of a ruin claiming to be the final home of Pythagoras. *OK, i'll go there too.*

We decided to set up a rough itinerary but leave most activities to the dictates of spirit, believing

141

that we would be guided to the important stuff. Exhausted, grimy and hungry, we arrived in Cortona. The travel guide boasted of a night in the convent on the top of the hill. That didn't happen. Discouraged and resigned to sleeping in the car, i heard the whisper, "Walk down into the town. Pay attention." Standing on the side-walk i noted two women across the street, when suddenly the voice said, "Ask them." We bustled across the street. In my practiced Italian, i asked if they knew of anywhere we could find a room for a couple of nights. "Yes, of course, follow us."

They led us to a building that housed students from the University of Georgia. It was a hostel-type affair that looked like a castle to two weary travelers. i placed our bags down, checked the water situation in the shower and went to the windows.

i opened the wooden shutters to behold a grand church. At that very instant the Bells of Cortona began filling the air. Tears flooded my eyes as i sensed the countryside saying 'Welcome to Italy.'

Everywhere we went in Tuscany, i felt right at home like I had returned from being abroad for a few years. The sounds and aromas, the emotional ambiance of the locals and the flow of everyday life seemed so familiar to me. Part of me resonated with the energy in each church i visited. Many of their frescos left me awestruck. i had no doubt that i lived there at one point in another lifetime.

We visited friends who maintained a home in the upper village of Baggio.

It was in this little village next to a section of the ancient Apian Way that i re-discovered the wonder of olive oil. i couldn't enough of it.
i brought five bottles back to the US.

St. Francis of Assisi

After Tuscany we headed for the province of Chianti. We settled into a hillside hotel before making the first trip to the Iglesia (church) where St. Francis spent his final years. i sat in a cave-type room where he slept. i chanted. The sound was alive as it bounced off the rock walls.

143

We entered the room where he received the stigmata, now a small, ornate chapel with pews lining the walls on three sides. We sat for no longer than five minutes when a priest told us that we had to leave the chapel. As we started walking away an inner voice said, "Stay here and wait."

i encouraged my companion to sit on the only bench in the area.

Within a matter of moments the sounds of Gregorian chanting filled the stone passage way. A number of monks in brown robes passed us on their way to the chapel.

They entered the chapel, chanted for ten minutes and left the same way they came – the sound of their voices trailing behind them. For me, that was a priceless moment.

The following day we took the advice of the hotelier and walked the ancient path up the mountain as pilgrims had done in the past. The rain was steady but light. After walking fifty yards, a black cat appeared out of nowhere, walked right over to me and began rubbing against my

pant leg. 'A cat (a black cat, no less) in the rain and making contact' – what significance did this have?

The cat never left my side until we entered the lower archway into the site. At a juncture in the path, i turned left in order to take some photos of an interesting statue. The cat literally screamed at me, telling me inwardly, "That's the wrong way. What are you doing? You have to go this way." After taking the shot and rejoining this strange feline, it calmed down and continued upward on the old path.

Once we reached the ancient stone archway, my little guide appeared satisfied that he/she had completed its mission.

During my visit to this site, i felt a strong presence close at hand. Something inside me felt completed as though all i had to do was physically be present while the cells within me were re-arranged. It felt magnetic to me. Was the spirit of St Francis present? i have no idea other than i knew my need to visit there was satisfied.

Padre Pio

The Padre Pio Sanctuary is located in San Gio-
vanni Rotondo. It is the place where the priest,
or monk, was said to have healed many people. Today this site of pilgrimage hosts some
fifty hotels and a large number of banks. Padre
Pio is a thriving, revenue producing business.
Even though the history was remarkable, i felt
let down by the experience. As i drove out of
town i remember thinking, "Is there anything
that isn't for sale?"

We found a hotel (a pink one in fact), had dinner and retired to bed. i felt discouraged as i
drifted off to sleep.

During the night i dreamt of meeting a priest
in an old monastery. He told me the secret of
healing. He said, "Always remember that true
healing comes from Divine Love. That is the
key. Keep your heart open to this Love. It will
work through you as long as you remain pure
of heart." When i awoke, i realized that i had
received a gift.

Did Padre Pio visit me in my dream? i don't really know, but whoever it was, left me an important piece of wisdom to live and work with.

Pythagoras

The next stop on the journey was Metaponto. The temperature was hot and dry; the food not to my liking and the people rather unfriendly. It seemed as though we hit all the people on a bad day. Despite our getting lost, we finally discovered the ruins of Pythagoras.

We sat next to a set of pillars and chanted for a while. As hard as i tried, i didn't experience any revelation or vision; just a feeling that 'something' was there. i wanted something — anything to happen. We had just driven clear across the country for what?

That evening i repeatedly apologized to my companion, telling her how sorry i was for putting us through so much misery for the past two days. Why did it seem so important for me to drag us to this place? What was i hoping to find? Questions ran through my mind as i closed my eyes.

i awoke in the dream state to find myself in a huge round ballroom with twelve very large people sitting on elevated dais-like chairs. Elegantly dressed and adorned with crowns, they sat overlooking the activities happening in the room. One of them suddenly arose and began dancing with a commoner who gazed at their regal partner with awe.

A voice beside me said, "These are the gods of Olympus. Whatever you do, do not look into their eyes or listen to their words. If you do so, you will become hypnotized and a slave to their whims."

One of the women left her seat, floated over to me and commanded me to dance. i heeded the warning of the voice, keeping my wits about me. As i did so i sensed a power emanating from the woman. She wanted to ensnare me yet did not succeed. Eventually, she gave up and returned to her chair. i realized a subtle truth – never consciously give away my freedom.

Once i received the lesson, i was instantly transported to a desert area. Next to me appeared

a man wearing an Indiana Jones type hat and dusty, yet clean clothes. His eyes were bright and filled with an ancient wisdom. He proceeded to instruct me in building a water distiller from simple objects.

As he taught me he said, "From now on you will be capable of creating water from its Divine source. This will create independence within you." His smile lit up the world around me. i woke up filled with love and gratitude and wrote down the dream. This was what i came to Metaponto for.

Rome

i recognized everything in Rome including the Vatican. It felt as though i had been there a hundred times. Even little things seemed familiar to me.

i wanted to stand inside the Forum, but as we approached the structure, i heard screams and felt such misery that i couldn't get near it. All i wanted was to get as far away as i could.

Vatican

The statues within the Vatican held no surprises for me. My companion told me that she felt 'creeped out' and had to leave the building. Without a thought i said, "Don't you know that it is all about power here?" She left while i wandered. i remember thinking as i stood in front of one papal statue, *Is it only about power? Didn't any of these leaders serve out of pure Love for God or was it all about ego?*

i came upon the last statue before the exit. A man was on his knees, hands clasped in prayer. Yes, i thought, *there are those who do what they do because of a profound Love for God. That is the way it should be.* i left the building.

After viewing the Pantheon, we stepped outside. She wanted to watch some procession so we agreed to meet later right where we stood.

When she walked off, i let my attention wander. My gaze settled upon an obelisk which supported an elephant on top. My first thought was,

Oh, an elephant, my sister Lizzie would like that.
Immediately my attention was pulled toward a
small church. The inner voice whispered, "Go
inside."

More of a large chapel than a church, the building contained a number of frescoes lining its
walls. i felt very comfortable inside. i walked
down the left side and back on the right, stopping at each nook to view the paintings. They
all looked vaguely familiar. The last fresco captured my complete and undivided attention. i
stood there for at least ten minutes captivated
by a painting of an angelic female. i couldn't
pull my gaze away. Tears started filling my
eyes. Suddenly i sensed a presence. i turned to
find an old priest standing next to me.

We both automatically stretched out our hands
in greeting.

We stood for a moment or three holding each
other's hand and staring deeply from eye to
eye. My heart began to open. i felt our hearts
connecting as well as the core of our beings
(soul to soul). When we released our grasps, we

both were shedding tears. Realizing that words couldn't hold what we experienced, we said nothing.

Simultaneously, we placed a hand on our respective hearts – we both knew that we had been touched by something special. My heart full, i left the building.

A Couple of Thoughts

What began as a romantic trip to Italia unfolded into a spiritual adventure.

i arranged the general itinerary, but inner wisdom led me directly to the events i needed to experience. All i had to do was arrive at the physical location, listen to the dictates of inner guidance or intuition and Spirit did the rest. By the time i returned home to Maine, another chapter of my ancient history integrated with the present lifetime. i didn't feel changed; i felt more complete, more whole, more of myself.

As with all of the above stories, intuition is a constant companion that guides us no matter where we happen to be or what we are doing. it is always with us.

CHAPTER TEN

Events That Enrich Our Lives

Life can be so drab unless we dive right into each day. When we view existence as something we must endure or take control of, we miss the magic that is hiding right in front of us. Many of us regret not taking those opportunities that come our way. They appear to us like doorways, stay open for a short while, then fade away into the past. We have to make a choice when the portal opens.

Whether we choose to follow the clue or intuitive message is always up to us. If we let it go, it is usually gone forever.

Consider for a moment that these opportunities for experience are presented to us because we are ready for them. No matter how profound or simple the event may be, the chance is provided for us to experience something. The big ones are difficult to miss. For example, when we meet our future spouse for the first time or an employment opportunity falls into our lap.

The smaller events are more subtle and require that we pay close and consistent attention to our immediate surroundings.

Let's say, for example, that you are in an airport awaiting your flight. You notice an elderly woman in one of those airport wheelchairs. She looks concerned as she unsuccessfully attempts to capture the attention of the person at the gate counter.

You are presented with a choice: do you assist her or let it go? You decide to walk over and ask

if she needs help. She tells you that she is worried about her flight not being on time because her daughter is waiting at her destination.

You go to the gate counter, gather the necessary information and return to the woman. The worry disappears from her face immediately. She thanks you profusely. You notice her eyes as they settle on the coffee you are holding. You are faced with another decision.

You decide to ask the woman, "Would you like a cup of coffee?" Her face lights up. "I would love a cup," she says. "Here, let me give you some money." You respond with, "It is my treat."

You return with the java and present it to the woman whose expression is nothing like that of the elderly lady you first noted.

You made her moment and all it cost you was a little bit of time and a cup o' Joe. She is happy and you are uplifted by the fact that you gave of yourself without any thought of return.

Therein harbors one of the keys to living: giving

without thought of return. We give to life and its inhabitants because we want to, not because we are building good karma, or doing good deeds. It becomes part and parcel of who we are.

To develop this attitude of giving, we must learn to pay attention to those around us. The focus changes from 'what is here for me' to 'how can i be of service to life.' Once we begin to live this way, we are no longer the center of our universe, but a channel for the Universe Itself.

The experiences and events that follow have added a little bit of magic to life no matter where I found myself.

AN UNLIKELY COMPANION AND KIDS ON THE CORNER

During my military tour in Vietnam i spent six months in NhaTrang, the second largest city in the country. Whenever i could i left the base and visited the town. There i explored many of the back streets and alleyways. My limited vocabulary helped me from getting utterly lost on numerous occasions.

A favorite spot of mine put me on a busy street corner outside a small store. My first time there, i saw an old man sitting on the sidewalk.

He smiled at me and said "Hi." I returned the greeting and entered the store. i received a little hunch, so i followed it and bought two Cokes and a loaf of French bread.

i returned to the sidewalk, sat down and offered the man a Coke and some bread. He seemed to appreciate it and said, "Thanks." As we sat there munching and sipping away, we watched the people coming and going.

Before we knew it, we created a scale of coolness and began rating the passersby from 1 to 10 (number 1 being the best and 10 being the lamest). We had a ball. Here we were, two strangers from completely different worlds, sitting on a street corner, checking out the locals and laughing up a storm.

i shared that small piece of real estate with the old guy five or six times. A tall, twenty-one year old blonde GI in a green military uniform and

a short, seventy-something Vietnamese man hanging out on a sidewalk.

Friendliness and companionship are capable of melting both language and cultural barriers anywhere in the world.

i grew accustomed to one route through the alleys. At one corner i discovered a young girl and boy playing a game on the ground using two short sticks and one stone. They were going right at it as kids typically do. i watched for a few moments.

Out in front of a shack-like house was a glass counter that held candy, cigarettes and other articles for sale. i greeted the man behind the counter and shook his hand. Next, upon a whim, i purchased some candy and split it with the two kids. i continued on my way.

Each time i took that route, i stopped, bought some candy and shared it with the boy and girl. One day, the guy who operated the little store, took me by the arm while waving me towards the house.

i remembered thinking, "Oh no, he's going to take me in the house, kill me and dump my body into the river. i shouldn't be out here all by myself."

Once at the door, he motioned for me to remove my shoes and follow him into the building. We entered the house where he introduced me to his wife and invited me to have lunch with her and the children (the kids in the alley).

The whole family seemed both friendly and curious about this man in green with yellow hair. They had no silverware – they scooped the rice from the bowls with their fingers. Proudly, they offered what they had. i attempted to explain that this rarely happened in my country, but my vocabulary distorted the message.

After finishing the green tea and a cookie, i thanked my hosts and walked off down the alleyway.

The experience left me feeling hopeful and believing that basic kindness does exist in the world – even in a war-torn country.

THE KIDS WITH THE EYES

I put the pack on, jumped on my Sears, one speed bike and rode the mile or so to the Haleiwa Health food store on the north shore of Oahu. i needed some stevia and quinoa; my supplies were low at the house. i spent about ten minutes searching the store before asking the woman by the counter for help.

She told me where to look.

i stooped down to find the quinoa on the bottom shelf of a rack. As i made my selection, i felt a strong presence behind me. i turned around and there he was – a 2 or 3 year old boy with huge blue eyes boring deep into me. i returned the gaze. We were locked together eye to eye. i winked at him and said, "Well, hi there." His whole face lit up. You know the look – a beam of inner brightness that melts your heart and fills the soul. The whole event lasted 3 or 4 seconds before his dad dragged him off to another part of the store.

Once at the counter with my goods, i decided

that i may as well buy some amaranth while i was there. Bent over at the same rack, i felt the same presence. Sure enough, there he was again. This time we connected, i felt a surge of energy flow through me and into the boy. The blast was strong enough to knock him onto his butt. He went down but his eyes never left mine.

His father picked him up, looked at me as if to say, 'what are you doing to my kid?' and headed for the exit. On the way out the door, the boy beamed me another smile as well as a wave goodbye. Still sensing the exchange of energy between me and the kid, i felt a blessed by the brief encounter as i climbed back on my bike and began pedaling home.

RAISING THE ROOF

Ten to twelve friends showed up that morning to help me raise and secure the roof rafters on my house.

There were sixteen long, heavy rafters in total; so heavy ,in fact, that i hired a truck with a crane to lift them to the second floor. Everyone

had specific jobs to do from centering and nailing down the rafters to providing the workers with food and drink.

A few days before the event, i felt a nudge to invite an older woman from the neighborhood (let's call her Arlene). She prepared a hearty, delicious soup for lunch. A ten year old boy handed out nails to the men on ladders.

Everything went smoothly and quickly. The feeling of warmth and companionship was palpable. What could have been an all day job was completed in just four and a half hours. The crane owner/operator told me that he had worked with many contractors but had never witnessed such caring and giving as he did that day. He felt it necessary to contribute something, so he charged me only half of his travel fee. How often does that happen in the construction world?

Later on in the afternoon, when people started to gather their tools and go home, i noticed Arlene giving each person a warm hug goodbye. When all of them left i walked Arlene to her car.

i said, "Thank you very much for your help and the wonderful soup."

She put her soup pot in the car and turned to face me. She replied, "No, Bob, thank you. Since my husband died two months ago I have felt so alone. Today was the first time since then, I have felt wanted and needed. There was so much love here that I feel full. This has been a beautiful experience for me. Thank you again." She gave me a sweet hug, climbed into her car and drove off.

Before walking back to the old house, i took a few moments to stand before my home to be, resplendent with brand new roof rafters. i swear i could see light and feel love emanating from its stick walls.

THE PEARLS

My auntie loved going to yard sales and flea markets. i rented an apartment in her house in Waialua on the north shore of Oahu. Along with paying rent, i agreed to drive her wherever she wished to go.

One Saturday morning she informed me that she wanted to visit the flea market at the Sunset Elementary School. A rather small affair, the market held about twenty tables including local food vendors. It took us less than forty five minutes to visit each and every table.

Before leaving, auntie stated that she wished to re-visit a particular jewelry vendor. i stood at one end of a table, rather bored, when my attention landed on a necklace of black pearls. The woman vendor noticed my interest and stated, "That necklace is sold, however, I will have more within two or three weeks. If you are interested in pearls, you'll love this."

She placed a necklace of orange-pinkish pearls on the table. They were stunning.

"These are undyed cultivated pearls and rather hard to come by. I can give them to you at an excellent price."

Immediately i thought; what am i doing? Right on cue the whisper sounded in my ear, 'Buy the pearls.' *This is nuts*, I thought. *What am i going to*

164

do with a pearl necklace? The voice commanded, 'Buy that one and order a black one as well.'

OK, *alright, i'll buy them*, i said to the inner voice. In a matter of moments i became the no-so-proud owner of a pearl necklace. i also ordered a black one. Worst case scenario – i could give them to my daughter or a sister for a special occasion. My auntie didn't buy anything; she laughed at me. Our business, concluded we drove home. i put the necklace in a drawer and let the matter go. There is usually a reason why i get these nudges but this one was definitely strange.

About a week or two later, a female friend landed in Hawaii. We met at a seminar the previous October and had been communicating for three or four months via e-mails and Skype.

i had absolutely no idea where or how the relationship would evolve; i had no real expectations other than getting to know this woman. i invited her for a visit to Oahu before our flight to Kauai to attend a campout retreat sponsored by our spiritual organization.

i greeted her at the airport in the traditional manner – a flower lei and a kiss on the cheek. Over the next few days i introduced her to the island including a glider ride over Ka'ena Point, a visit to a heiau (Hawaiian sacred shrine) and a day drive around the island.

One evening while preparing to visit the Polynesian Culture Center, inner guidance came to my attention telling me, 'Give her the necklace.' *What? i thought.* 'Give her the necklace right now,' it repeated. *OK.*

i went to the drawer, pulled it out, took a deep breath and walked out into the other room where she was seated at the table. i remember thinking, *how do i do this?; what do i say?* 'Trust, and speak from your heart' was all it said.

i sat in front of her, nervous and not knowing where to start. She looked at me with a question in her eye. i opened both my heart and mouth and spoke. i told her i had no idea why she was there or what this relationship was all about. However, she has flown across two oceans and a large continent to spend this time with me.

"Inner guidance is telling me to give you this gift. No matter what happens, i am glad that you are here." i placed it around her neck; she gave me a hug. Tears filled our eyes.

Our relationship has grown for over four years now. She also has the black pearl necklace.

A LAST THOUGHT

i cannot possibly imagine what my life would be like without the influence of intuition or inner guidance.

The stories provided within these pages are but a smattering of the events i have experienced over the years. i am not that different from everyone else who lives here.

i have the same concerns, fears and wishes that all people have. Like so many of us, i've had my share of mistakes and poor choices.

If anything in particular singles me out, it is the fact that i have listened to and followed the dictates of inner wisdom at almost every turn.

No matter how simple or profound the piece of information, i have trusted its guidance and acted upon it. Though some of the directives have been difficult for me to accept at first, IT has never failed me.

A few years back, i sat on a back porch with a man for whom i have great respect.

With a genuine look, he asked, "Bob, how are you? What is happening in your life right now?" i pondered the question for a moment or two and replied. "i feel like i am twelve years old again.

You know, that age where i can be curious, somewhat mischievous and excited about life at the same time. i have come to the realization that all Life around me is talking and i am beginning to understand some of Its language. My life has become magical again like that of a child and i am forever grateful for the opportunity to be part of IT."

What else can i say other than thank you for your attention? i sincerely hope that you carry away something you can use in your life from reading these pages. Until we meet again ...

About The Author

Born on Miami Beach in the middle of a hurricane, Robert Munster's life has been a whirlwind from the get-go. Moving from Florida with his family of five siblings, he spent his formative years in Maine. After being drafted and spending a year in Vietnam, Robert has lived a nomadic lifestyle in response to inner guidance. Having resided in Massachusetts, Michigan, California, Oregon, Nevada, Montana, Utah, and Hawaii, he continues that trend by splitting his time between the Dominican Republic and Maine.

Mr. Munster has spent thirty five years as an Occupational Therapist working in numerous medically related settings including acute and long term rehabilitation, home health, schools

and private practice. He continues to participate in multi-hands therapy programs utilizing inter-species communication and behavior to promote the healing process.

During the summers Robert Munster lives in his sixteensided, two-story home in the middle of the Maine woods.

Not far from the Atlantic, Robert loves to spend time in his gardens growing vegetables, fruits, flowers and medicinal herbs.

When not gardening, writing, editing or involved in building projects, you will find him engaged in varied, outdoor activities.

These include kayaking, surfing, biking, picking wild fruit or hunting edible mushrooms in the mountains and forests.

When not surfing or writing, Robert spends the winter months involved in sustainable agriculture and creating educational programs. In between and around his many projects, he always finds the time for a trip to snow covered

mountains or a new country. In alignment with his lifestyle, Robert is presently an editor and travel writer for *The Vacation Rental Travel Guide.*

Robert lives with his sweetheart and regularly visits his children and grandchildren who reside in California. Nicknamed Duay, Robert spends as many hours as possible hanging out with the kids doing whatever comes up. Sending the parents away for a night or a weekend, Duay and the crew can be found partying up a storm, watching a show and eating ice cream or popcorn until the wee hours of 8:30 pm.

Other Inspired Living Books

Made in the USA
Lexington, KY
10 October 2014